HOW TO THANK YOUR
FATHER

Already Published:

Spiritual Growth in the Midst of Challenges: A
positive Answer To A Destructive Disposition

HOW TO THANK YOUR
FATHER

The deeds of your Parents and your Lineages

Adolfo Makuntima

 authorHOUSE®

AuthorHouse™ LLC
1663 Liberty Drive
Bloomington, IN 47403
www.authorhouse.com
Phone: 1-800-839-8640

Published by AuthorHouse   02/14/2014

ISBN: 978-1-4918-6371-8 (sc)
ISBN: 978-1-4918-6372-5 (hc)
ISBN: 978-1-4918-6373-2 (e)

Library of Congress Control Number: 2014902937

KJV—King James Version
Scripture taken from the King James Version of the Bible.

CONTENTS

DEDICATION

Here we are in our second publication; many of those who read our first publication did not hesitate to voice their opinions about the entire process, especially the editorial aspect that was not very well done. We thank you for your advises, attention and your love. If the content was astonishing to many, the absence of the links between the topics did escape the praise of some readers. We are working with less financial means and we are our own author, secretary, and first editor. All we wish is that the team that will be working on this publication may have your concerns in their hearts and learn from past mistakes in order to improve our working relationship and our brand.

We thank Jean Martin Mabozi (Congolese) and brother Anthony (from Ghana) for the technical advises; we also thank those who could help but were prevented to do so by some inconveniences; We thank George (from Uganda) who, after he was told about the title of this book, did not hold his breath to declare that many of our African youths of Toronto/Canada are serving time in prisons because of the lack of interactions in the family; there is no more time of serious dialogues between African parents and their children.

We thank our family members who always wish us the best; especially my daughter Sarah N'Kenge Rivard; I would like you to know that (Daddy), your Father is trying very hard to preserve the great conscience and memories of our Ancestors.

Thanks to my mother Marie-Josee Diabanza Diambi and to my father Antoine Tukilonga Tekadiomona.

To my brothers and sisters, nephews and nieces thank you for your love and your prayers.

Great Spirit, We thank you for giving us the Greatest Mama Nzinga,

the Queen of Queens who announced since the third century the coming of the Ntumua Kimbangu, not just for the Kongolese of Kongo Kingdom, but for all Black generations in the world;

Great Spirit, we thank you for the presence of Ntumua Kimbangu among our great fathers and our Fathers. And among us, who (Kimbangu) came to give dignity to the black men and women of this world, and for the many wonders he did, which were seen and verified, and can still be seen to these days;

Great Spirit of Kongo Katiopa, Kemet or Kamite also known today as Africa. We thank you for sending us the great multi-disciplinary and the polyvalent scientist Cheikh Anta Diop, who silenced the entire world with his intellectual findings and who revived into black People, the Creative Spirit that was suppressed and induced to sleep by the Europeans;

Great Spirit, we thank you for giving us still to these days Professors Theophile Obenga, Coovi Gomez, Molefi Asante, Pastor and Doctor Ray Hagins, Papa Nkusu and Mbombog Mbog Bassong who are TEACHING THE NEW GENERATION OF AFRICANS that Euro-Centric teaching is based on falsifications. Therefore, we Africans need to go back to our Ancestral ways of Teaching and dig deeply the true and right knowledge, the only way to our Salvation;

Finally, Great Spirit, I thank you for giving me excellent parents, Mama Diabanza Diambi and Tata Tukilonga, who shaped my intellectual and spiritual life. Thank you for leading me to share these few pages with the world, as imperfect they could be, let those who read them find wisdom and guidance in their lives.

PREFACE

More than once I reflected on (Africa), Kongo Katiopa, Kamite or Kemit, the true names of the Mother Continent, I always try to see if that Continent is really finished. No, No, I always answer. There is more we can learn from this part of the world; especially now that all eyes are turning towards the land of life and secure opportunity. Its nature alone is Godly and as Spinoza said: "God and Nature are the same. Knowing nature is for sure, knowing God Himself." When that time comes when I really have to think about Africa, my memories of yesterday bring desires of going back to my infancy. Why? Because I now know and realize that my being was shaped there during that period.

I remember my mother and father putting a piece of tree on the top main door of our house. They told us that that tree protects against thunders and tornadoes, but it really was Nsanda Tree, the tree of Truth. Who ever is bounded with that tree will speak the truth. And you can only find that tree in the Kongo Kingdom (zaire, Angola, Gabon and Congo Brazza Ville). In the course of my life, I could not figure out why whenever I want to tell a lie, I always ended up speaking the truth. The answer is simple, Nsanda Tree. I am the Angel of the truth. This is why many weak minds are uncomfortable and hurt in their feelings just by being in my surroundings.

One day, at the school where I am teaching, my colleague (another French Teacher) took a day off and the board sent a supply teacher, a blond lady in her 50's or 60's, pronounced my name and said that I Makuntima was an Enigma. I did not bother asking her why she said that. Someone I did not know, who never lived nor worked with me before, was calling me an enigma. I only said: white people talk among themselves about one single of us. It was later on that I learned from my colleague that that supply teacher was a retired, was my colleague's mentor, and always enjoyed talking with principals. This fact alone reinforces my notion that white people study Africans more than themselves.

And I also know that even thought they analyze us (blacks), in contrary, they certainly do not know themselves. And when they cannot comprehend somebody deeply, they start explaining them with adjectives and mere weird words. If I said that some of them in this city (where I am living) are after me, I will sound sick. But the truth is my truth hurt them. After they have planned every evil operation to cripple me and they failed, I become an enigma. The quote I love most is the one that was said about Saint Peter and his fellow Apostles by Gamaliel to the Sanhedrins: **"Leave this guy alone if his enterprise is human, it will collapse but if it is from God, do not take a risk to combat against God"** (Acts 5:38-39).

I always thought of writing this Biblical quote and hanging it in my office, but I restrained not to open the door to the enemies. Sometimes you have to ignore your enemies in order to make them become more confused. But the quote I am bearing is the following: **"Do not approach me or come near me if you do not like or support the truth."** In fact, we (human beings) all know something and have something to say; it is just to find a way to say it, this I was told by father Ezeogu. And the great Historian of our time, Professor Coovi Gomez was told by The ever Great Savvy Cheikh Anta Diop that knowledge is largely wide like an ocean, you cannot take the entire water, just take your buckle and get the quantity of water you need or can. I am writing this book to share the portion of knowledge I possess if you like it, fine if you do not, I think you can at least guess the language I would like to use here . . .

"THE ONLY PEOPLE WHO ARE MAD AT YOU FOR SPEAKING THE TRUTH ARE THOSE PEOPLE WHO ARE LIVING A LIE. KEEP SPEAKING THE TRUTH"

En Afrique plus qu'ailleurs, nous marchons sur notre passé enfoui. La majeure partie de l'histoire africaine est enterree et pour interroger serieusement le passé de ce continent, il faut descendre sous terre. Mais il ne faut pas y descendre

sans guide ni en desordre, car quand on ne sait pas ce qu'on cherche, on ne comprend pas ce qu'on trouve.[1]

In Africa, more than anywhere else on Earth,
We tread over our buried past.
The major part of African History is buried
And in order to seriously find out the History
Of this continent, we must dig underground.
However, we should not go down there without
Guidance or in disorder because "When you do
Not know what you are looking for, you cannot
Understand what you find.[2]

In Africa more than elsewhere, we walk over our past buried. The most part of African history is underground and to seriously question the past of this continent, it is necessary to dig down subterranean. But you should not dig down there without guide nor in disorder, because when you do not know what you search, you do not understand what you find.[3]

I took this quotation from KIZERBO, an African Historian who was considered a sell out by many. But the merit of its content is indisputable because it tells the fact as it is. Far from taking the side of an historian, a field where we know a lot (based on the new founding by a great team lead by Professor Coovi Gomez), but where we could also tumble and trip for the lack of expertise and methodology, we feel that it is in our interest to bring to light what we are going to explore in the fields we know le moins mal, (least bad), Sociology and Anthropology or even Philosophy and Theology.

The world is not stranger to the writings of Cheikh Anta Diop, especially his Thesis for one of his Sociological Themes about Matriarchy and Patriarchy systems. Many years ago, someone posted on the Internet the audio component of the defense of that Doctorate Thesis. I used to

---

[1]   Joseph Ki-zerbo, *Histoire de l'Afrique noire, d'hier à demain* (Paris: Editions Hatier, 1972), 39.

[2]   Ibid [my own translation].

[3]   Ibid.

listen to it whenever I got some free time; and I was wondering why in the World, Diop would choose such a Topic?

Now I fully know and understand. Anta Diop wanted to get us back to the roots, the center of the African roots that is the family where we belong. Everything became clear when I read: The Instruction of Ptah-Hotep and Instruction of Ke'Gemni, the most old book in the world. This book, as a two pages, extracted from the soil and sands of the Ancient Old Black Egypt, is the pivot of the entire book of Wisdom and Proverbs we read today in the Bible. My joy was immense to find out that this book was in the residency of any human beings intellectual repertoire and belonging.

I recalled one radio host who is today a Principal of an elementary school in Canada, who at that time (in the early 90's) invited me and a friend who left this world (peace to his Soul), we both were called to that program because we were the leading French African Artists in Toronto, Canada music sphere. After the introduction to this radio program, the host played the SONG KAMIKI, well known by Congolese and Africans (just to remind you that this host was not from the Congo, he was from Uganda), but managed through music to learn the LINGALA language, simply because Congolese music conquered the entire Continent of Africa. In that song, you could hear the singer's tone:

. . . Kamiki yeye Motema ha, (2X)
Ba boti ba yebaka Testament,
Ba boti, bayeba ntango mateya,
Kamiki nasengi, Totosa nde baboti . . .
"Kamiki my heart, my love; . . . our parents knew the (history) past,
our parents knew when to teach . . . , Kamiki I am begging you to
listen to our parents . . .
This song revemps the quotation we wrote above. Similarly to
another African adage that always says:
"When an old man died, it is an entire library that is gone . . . " [4]

This notion of reverence to grandparents and parents was hidden to us

---

[4]   Amadou Hampate Ba, French African author.

by those who ripped Africa from it pride and by those who colonized the mother continent, simply because they wanted us to become lost. They wanted us to be cut off from our rich and uncontestable (legacy) heritage; but they have FORGOTTEN that the underground of Africa would speak to the point that it becomes the source of our continuous revelation. Now, we know better who we were, who we are and who we are going to be. This is why we decided to write about parents by not keeping the promise we made in our first book which consisted of writing on prayers, which it seems minimal and insignificant when we know for sure that the True and Great prayer is not what you read from somebody else hand-writing but the one that comes from your own heart and mind and the one you said your self with your mouth. So, knowing where you come from, who you are and who brought you here to this world, appears more meaningful than what we anticipated.

INTRODUCTION

We are living in dangerous time when some fathers and mothers are seen and perceived as bad fathers; bad mothers and some as good fathers; good mothers. Hearing the cries of many, we must accept that many fathers have done terrible things to their children, and beside those bad fathers, we must also have the courage to recognize fathers and mothers who have distinguished themselves by positively impacting their children by giving them the best affection and the attaining education a loving father or mother can offer. To appreciate the work they have done in our lives, we need to know who these parents are; what they represent in society and in what way and angles they are marking our beings.

Our goal here is neither to make one feels guilty nor defend any fathers. Instead, we are inviting the children of the world to open their eyes and look, and try to see, in their lives, if they could find a father like mine who was sometimes present and sometimes absent in my life, but managed to shape, in a good way, my personality and empower my existence, without me losing the person I am.

Blessed is one who sits in the hands of Amen Ra,

For it is He who directs the timid, who rescues the humble and the needy, who gives the breath of life to the one whom He loves and grants him or her a long life in West of Thebes.

Oh my God, Lord of Lords, Amen Ra, Lord of Karnak. Give me your hand and save me. Shine upon me and sustain me. You are the only God and there is none like you. You are Ra who rises in heavens, the God who created men and women.

It is you who hears the prayers of one who calls on Him, who saves a man and woman from the hands of the violent and who makes the Nile rise and flow for those who are in Him. Ra is the perfect guide for everyone.

When He rises men and women live and their hearts are lifted up when they see the one who gives the breath of life to those who are in the egg. Who make people and birds to live, who supplies even food for mice in their holes as well as for worms and fleas.

May He grant us an honorable burial after an old age, so that we may be safe in His hands.[5]

Prayer of Amenomope and his wife Hathor. (The HUSIA)

---

[5]   Maulana Karenga, *Selections from The Husia, Sacred Wisdom of ancient Egypt* (Los Angeles: The university of Sankore, Press Los Angeles 1984), 1.5

CHAPTER 1
MY FATHER

As it used to happen very often when our father has to leave us in Kinshasa the capital of Congo, to go do business (buying) merchandises in the Bas-Congo province where he also had two or three wives, (les Africains comprennent la polygamie, mais ils ne tolerent pas l'adultere)= (Africans understand polygamy but do not tolerate adultery). We would be left alone with our mother and she would do her best with her grocery commerce (selling) vegetables and fruits, in order to feed us. We were 8 children from the same father and mother but later on we lost one of our sisters, the lastborn.

In situations like these ones, I would seek help from members of the family from the large side family of my father. One day, I went to pay a few days visit to my cousin, the big brother, a son of my paternal uncle. I arrived in the evening. We spent the night and the following morning, while I was sitting on the chair in the yard and each one other has his spot, the youngest cousin, a son of my same uncle came to me with a jar of water; he knelt down on my feet and started washing my feet. Surprised I was, I said in my inner being this is the scene described in the Bible; Jesus washing the feet of his disciples, a sign of humility and a sign of love (as we have been told). Why this cousin is doing this to me?

I had no clue and I let him clean my feet and dry them with the towel. As the family was gathering, one of my cousins, the second big one, asked me the following question: Do you really know your father? I was there smiling and that was my way of answering people who seems suspect to me. And then in the gathering of all the members of the family, especially from the Father side, I replied why are you asking me that question. Then that cousin spoke to me and said: your Father has a healing power. Whenever he goes to the province, when he enters the village, people who knew him will bring gifts to him; those who are sick will come to him for healing and your father will pray for them and they will get well. Then

I knew why that cousin came to wash my feet It was by respect of the deeds and power of my father not my ambition of going to the Catholic Seminary and becoming a Priest. I firmly believed my cousins because they used to live in the village where those things used to happen.

Now I was aware of my father, but I knew that he was a man of prayers, in Kinshasa, when he was with us, no matter how the circumstances and the conditions of life looked like, he was day and night praying for the family. Sometimes we would pay attention and sometimes we would not but hear his voice praying in the diverse corners of our house. The house was so big and the work was not achieved. It was clear, our Father built the house in the hope of us the children to finish it and that in reality is what happened.

From that day on, I really knew who my father was, a spiritual and a businessman who wanted his children to go to school and learn and to shape their future for the best by their own efforts. Both father and mother used to tell us that a child must know the price of the bread before his parents are dead. Meaning that a child must be independent and not relying on any inheritance. He also used to tell my uncles, his brother that a child should not to be carried like an egg. The only great legacy was the preparation of mind and spirit my father settled and arranged for us.

In my previous book I explained how my father and mother saved me from two death experiences. It is because of their exploits, feats and bravery that I am still alive today.

In the course of my multiple one on one conversations, my father would come to me, because in my youth, (during my secondary school), I developed the habit of sitting or standing by the window almost every evening and night Just sitting or standing there alone thinking about life or recapitulating the lessons and courses I had memorized. I used to memorize books; from page one to the last page and sometimes I would call a friend to whom I would ask to open the page of the book and follow and listen to me repeating word by word of the book. At the end I would know for sure I was ready for the exam. I was at that time, as we said in Pedagogy; a full head and at the same time a well-done head. My Father would approach me and start giving me advice and wisdom in the term of palaver. He was so interesting, so wise in his parables, so captivating in his father to son dialogues. Most of the time I was smiling to see that he was really educating me and was really paying more attention to me. That became a routine. And I should not forget my mother who was doing the same in her time, but mostly she used to tell us stories of our family while we were eating. **Vana dia, vana longi.** Time to eat is the time to lecture and teach as her brother, my uncle, told her to practice on us as a ceremony like. So, she used to apply it to us at every meal.

That was the full initiation we were receiving because father always opposed the idea of us, his children going to the village. I realized this at the age of 48 year-old while living in Canada. How among the songs I was composing, one of the songs or may be three, were inspired by the teaching of my parents. So one day, when I discovered that one of the refrains of my songs was century or even a billionaire hold traditional rooted song of the Kongo Kingdom, I said yes mother was right. Father was right. I then understood the need to go to the village to learn the ways of the villagers because the village and the tradition were within us in the heart of Kinshasa, in our own family home.

I mention this fact to justify the reality that you know more than we your children could think and imagine. But make no mistake, Father I knew your power long ago. Everybody who trespassed against you ended up paying anyway. When we were very young Nkaka VEDI, the Kimbanguist Pastor come to our house Lemba to spend some spiritual time with you because you were having difficulties selling the same house where we were living, in the end the house was sold. I knew ceremonies were taking place; and on my own side I do not know how but I used to have dreams about cats. And when Grand Father, the one whose name I carry used to come to the Capital, he would take me to the Bar, la Source, still in Lemba, where he would tell me the story on how in bars in the villages, they attract women. Father you used to bless us with your saliva spit on our forth head, and lift us up in air in your both hands, practice many parent ignore today.

Mama, instead used to put animal bones and leafs and piece of tree and some coin money in the basin where she used to bath us in our infancy;

I could not forget all those things; they have strong meanings. Today when I think about life, I know how you both cared for us and blessed us. And you know we did not disappoint. But I must say that you know more and thought us little. Remember that in my forty I have to ask you the true name of our Ancestral God. When you told me the name of our real God, I had doubt, I though you were joking until later on I heard the same name from one of the great spiritual Congolese leader whom I also admire, I then said: my Father was right.

Now, especially when I am feeling like I have to put a stop on my music career, you told me like you already read my mind that I should not stop music. That was your recommendation. But many of the problems I have encountered in this adoptive country I am living in now is largely due to the music I love and I perform; not to mention my passion for school. I know, the late monsieur l'Abbe Mayivangua was right, a white man does not want to see a black intelligent man. And I do not know why, because yes knowledge is money, but it is also help. A friend of mine who is a Doctor told me, after I revealed to him that I am going to publish another book: ***HOW TO THANK MY FATHER***. I verbally gave him the synopsis. He told me if I can write a book explaining how I compose my songs, that will help many young people.

I could not answer him. He is from West Africa. In that part of the world, they believe people accomplish things mostly by cabalistic way, but I am KONGO and as you know Father, my grand grand-Father on my Mother's lineage carried the name SOBA YIMBILA; which means choose to sing. Singing is in my blood, maybe the inspirational songs I continually have comes from Him. Anyway, I will never disappoint you. But on many occasions you said nothing could bother us even after your death. You also always said very important things, I reserve the right to reveal in this book. The reality is that; most of the time I am attacked. I have nonsense challenges from people. But if something happened to me, when and where I cannot take revenge, Father I asked you to strike back, retaliate strongly. If I go to the other side before time, send them also, all of them with their children and wives.

This world, where I am living has shown me no mercy. Therefore, no pity should be theirs. I remember Father, in Linguala in Kinshasa, you cured one man who became your friend. You did it from **Makaya Mansi (the herbs of our country)**, but that friend of yours lost along the way one of his children. Daree was our friend, we went to the mourning night gathering where a ceremony of retaliation was carried on. I remember we were in secondary school, Daree was of our age, and was sent in the Province of Bandundu, where one day, he went to bath in the river 60 centimeters deep and ended up drowning. The enemy took his body and soul. But his family retaliated and in revenge, killed back nine people from the family of those who killed Daree.

Father, that is how you should act if something happened to me before my regular due time-oldness—. Terminate them all, you know the ways; you have the means. If you hesitated, Uncle will never hesitate, and meanwhile, the same way I fought them in the living, I will be hunting those bastards to their deaths here on earth and more when most of them will come to the other side, I will take care of them by making sure that they end up for good into the spiritual prisons of heaven. It sounds silly, but silly must be paid by silliness in order to stop jealousy and bad behaviors. The reader who might be struck by this statement needs to read **Schopenhauser** when he clearly said:

> *En ces jours de disillusion et de souffrances, les classes pauvres avaient pour la plupart la consolation des esperances religieuses; mais dans les classes superieures, beaucoup avaient perdu la foi et contemplaient un monde en ruines sans la vision consolatrice d'une vie plus haute dont la justice finale et la beaute feraient oublier ces maux et ces laideurs. Et en verite, il etait assez difficile de croire qu'une planete aussi triste que celle qui s'offrait aux hommes en 1818—en cette instance 2013 pour les Africains—fut soutenue par la main d'un Dieu intelligent et bon.*[6]

> *In these days of disillusion and of suffering, the poor classes had mostly the solace of the religious hopes; but in superiors classes, many people had lost faith and considered the world in ruins without the comforting vision of a higher life among which final justice and*

---

[6]   **Collectif,** Vies et Doctrines des grands philosophes (Pays: Editions, année), 335 [bold is mine].

5

*beauty would make forget these wrong and this hideousness. And
truly, it was rather difficult to think that a so sad planet as the one
that presented herself to the men in 1818—in this authority, 2013 for
the Africans, was supported by the hand of a clever and good God.*[7]

Prior to this piece, I asserted in my first book and repeated my mantra:
Let not the circumstances of this life change me. But now based on
the reality of life which is, as some philosophers and politicians said:
BAD, and the same notion of bad which I can, anyway, find in the
Kikongo language NZAMBI; NZA= World and MBI= Bad, meaning
that the—world is bad-; therefore, it is without a shadow of doubt that
we must all become Mauvais (Bad) and practice the eye for eye teeth for
teeth rule in order to gain respect and serious consideration. Other wise,
those who treat us bad and to whom we return nothing (as a retaliation)
will perpetually be laughing at us.

Was not Machiavelli right in his philosophy? And you do not have to
look very far back in history to see how in this world in our time some
politicians who used to be good at the beginning of their careers ended up
becoming awkward and evildoers because they had really enough of evil
deeds that were brought against their lives by other people. So, as a result,
they end up becoming bloodsuckers. Not putting aside or ruling out the
discourse of Chaka Zulu who once said: **"The absolute Power requires
the blood of the most important being . . . "** [8] Meaning the blood of
a human being. And this mostly applies to Magicians, witchdoctors,
business entrepreneurs, religious leaders and Politicians who are depend
on divers sacrifices in order to strengthen their positions just to forget the
true source of power and later to realize that they are being evil. It is really
sad when you can detect and observe their weird deeds.

"VANA LUZITU KWA FUENE LUZITU, VANA VUEZO KUA FUENE VUEZO"

"GIVE RESPECT TO THOSE WHO DESERVE IT AND DISDAIN TO WHERE IT IS REQUIERED" (Proverb of my Father).

---

[7]   Ibid [my own translation].

[8]   Shaka Zulu, volume 1. Collectif Africain. Zaire.

Do not get me wrong, The BaKongo people also stupile (in contradiction of the definition of NZA-MBI) that: **Nza ya Mbote kansi mavanga meto ma sueka ntima mavondele Nza**= The world is a good place, but the dueling hidden in our hearts is what it is killing the world. It is like I am really going here against the teachings of my Parents who insisted and urged me to do well all the times; no matter what, keep doing good things to people because we do not know where we come from, why we are living here and where we are going. I also have in mind the advice given to me by Papa Nkusu (a spiritual leader from Kongo): **Oyo alonaka mabe azuaka mpe mabe, oyo alonaka malamu a pikolaka mpe malamu.** (you reap what you sow). I am not departing from these teachings, but I am only changing my attitude vis-à-vis the people of bad intentions and hearts.

I know the maker of Heaven has sent us on this earth to love and cherish one another and to care for everyone as the Instruction of Ptah-Hotep and the Instruction of Ke'Gemni teach, in their domestic and social lives of the 'Old Kingdom.', **"We read of the wife, who must be treated kindly at all costs; the genial generosity of the rich man, and the scowling boor, a thorn in the side of his friends and relations, the laughing-stock of all men . . . "**[9] In the same sense of material welfare rewarding, as a matter of course, an honorable life. Following his reasoning, if a man be obedient as a son, punctilious as a servant, generous and gentle as a master, and courteous as a friend, then all good things shall fall to him. He shall reach a green old age honored by the King, and his memory shall be long in the land.[10] (P.31). Believe me I followed and practiced all of these theories and I have been living the wisdom of MAAT described in the book THE HUSIA, that the creator "Di.FAnkh" gives life; Human beings in turn must give that which sustains life—both mental and physical. (XI). And to continue the creator RA said:

"I made every person like his and her fellow; and I did not command them to do evil . . ."[11] which all of this symbolizes the sacred wisdom

---

[9]   *The Instruction of Ptah-Hotep and the Instruction of Ke'Gemni.* P.26

[10] Ibid., 31.

[11] Karenga Maulana, *Selections from The Husia, Sacred Wisdom of ancient Egypt,* 7.

of the Black man of our Ancestors which is not respected anymore; just to be replaced by Jean Jacques Rousseau's saying that:

"Humans (men and women) are born good but nature or environment make them Evil." Indeed we must save our race from playing the rules of the evil one; but I always question myself: if this is the case, what would be the rewards and fate of a good person on this Earth? Because it seems like evil people are living better lives compare to those who do the well . . .

So, the line to draw here is the following: Be good to those who are good to you and be very evil to those who are Evil. Amadou Hampate Ba put it clearly that:

> **O Wangrin! Mon ami! Quand un homme malpropre au moral et au physique te donne dans l'ombre un coup de pied, il faut lui en donner dix publiquement, sinon le salaud ira dire partout que la nature t'a prive de membres pour repondre.**[12]

> *O Wangrin! My friend! When a dirty man or woman in morale and in physical appearance gives you in (darkness) or shade a kick, it is necessary to give him ten publicly, otherwise the bastard will go to say everywhere that nature has deprived you members to struck back* [my own translation].

Needless, here, to tell you that those who control the rest of the population will voice their opinions just to tell you that this generation which the revolutionary spirit was suppressed and put to death by slavery, colonization, lynching with Willie lynch syndrome, and now by Christianity and Islam would get out there without purification kind of rituals to act out of that trauma and seek revenge as we are stating it here; or would in another word say this is not the way. They are totally and fully wrong. This is the way; I insist this is the way. The only way they control you is by asking you to restrain from your strong actions and from violence. They always convince you to remain calm and accepting any outcome. That is the way they control and submit you. You then

---

[12]   Amadou Hampate Ba, *L'Etrange Destin de Wangrin ou Les Roueries d'un interprete africain* (Union Generale des editions, 1973), 45.

become robots; here I cite for example the case of one basketball player who became gay. One of his friends wrote a twit message saying: why opt for this kind of life when America is full of beautiful women?

The twitter was harassed to the point that they forced him not just to remove his comment but also to apologize. Robot, a second example is one of the football-player who wrote a tweeted that the jury that acquitted George Zimmerman in the Trayvon Martin's case, should all go home and commit suicide, people rose up in asking the league to punish him. So, simple as we can hear it, no one should then express or speak his/her mind? Then accept that you are not free. Therefore you are really, really robots or may be you are like domestic animals. But remember that even domestic animals do not hesitate to attack when and after they have had enough of bad actions being inflicted on them. They aggress their owners. So, to the reader, feel proud very proud, to be human and always keep in mind that action speaks more than words and consequently you need to:

- — use your emotions;
- — release your power;
- — fight forcefully for your cause;
- — gain your respect;
- — seek revenge;
- — go for vengeance;
- — and win, win

It is possible. Yes, it is achievable. This is how the world will respect and fear you. I am not asking for the use of gun or knife; your magic power alone can end someone's bad and evil intention or behavior. Believe me there is a way; witchcraft[13] in the African ways for example. People (specialists) are there, waiting to perform ceremonies for you the victims to struck back against your aggressors.

---

[13] By witchcraft, we mean your African Gods, your Ancestral powers and Gods, your mystics; not like we see today that all the African leaders are following the Free Masons; Illuminati the white stole from the black Egyptians, and Rosecrucian which they are taking wrongly. Not the god of Whites and Arabs, in the persons of Jesus or Mohammed and not even Buddha or Adonai. No, No, Africans seek and follow the Gods of your Ancestors in the end you will see the outcome.

Chapter 2
Youth's Turbulence

Going back to my kindergarten, and to my elementary school where I was really brilliant, polite, calm, respectful, But brutal sometimes, my colleagues were cautious playing with me because sometime I did not care how physically big and strong they might look, I was skinny, but very intelligent and active in sport. One day one of my classmates embarrassed me with his joke; I got angry in the middle of the class, I stood up and slashed him on the face. The teacher was not there at that moment. The entire class was astonished and the strong boy who used to bully every body did not react on the spot but had promised a fight at the end of the school day. I did not know what to do, to run away or to stand for the fight? At that time in Kinshasa, school would start at 7:30 in the morning and end at 5:00 in the evening.

At the end of school day, on that particular day, the gang boy was there, but he did not come to me given his warnings. May be I became invisible or may be he was just afraid to confront me.

The other element was the fact that all my teachers at the elementary school were showing me deep reverence and respect. I was intelligent and coming mostly first or among the first five of the class. That was a Kimbanguist school in Lemba 1 in Kinshasa.

One period, I missed school due to a broken left arm, so one of my teachers came to pay me a visit. I was in the middle of eating my breakfast and the living room was not clean. I was happy to see my teacher coming to my house to know how I was doing but I was also ashamed that the house was not clean. Mother and father were not there that morning they had left for work. This kind of attention was very interpellator to me but at the adult age, while reflecting on those past memories, the answer came clear to my mind, I was Ma**kuntima;** the same name the Spiritual Leader of the Kimbanguist Church was caring Diangienda **Kuntima**, the Son of the Great Prophet, **NTUMUA** and GOD **KIMBANGU**. So, the respect was due by name, parallelism and similarity.

And let me tell you, in Africa, names have meanings, and they always define personality.

My name was Adolphe Makuntima Makwiza. Meaning that what will come is already in my heart; or the secret of the heart. And believe me, I used to see in dreams the exams I was going to write. And I would remember everything and write and pass the exams. Also, through dreams, I used to profess and predict many events in my family as well as those outside my family.

This apprehension developed my mind and my intellect and placement Secondary school was easy for me but due to the lack of economic means I failed my literature school, in one of the prestigious schools in the Democratic Republic of Congo at that time; then I switched to Pedagogy (Science of Teaching) where I operated wonders in psychology, biology, mathematic and pedagogy.

But the road was not easy economically speaking. Most of the time my father was away in the province. The lack of saving would leave us with almost nothing and there were times where I had to go to school with an empty stomach and with a pant with one or two holes but I did not give up studies. Nothing could prevent or stop me from going to school. I loved school more than anything else. It was also, during that adolescent period in secondary school where my mind was opened to KIMPA VITA and to the true meaning of some triangles thanks to the help of my friend and classmate MATUKIMINA, a very intelligent young student who came from the MAYONBE in the province of Bas-Zaire (lower West CONGO).

In fact we were three competitors, myself, Yoba Kambu Lievin who is today a Roman Catholic Priest in Kinshasa, and Matukimina whom I lost track of. And we have two terminal secondary classes, but Matukimina was in my class. If I was first of the class at the finishing exams, Matukimina would be second. If he was first of the class, I would be second in the final exam and it was like that every semester from grade 9 to grade 13. It was a pacific intellectual emulation. Yoba Kambu instead was always first in his class, but was a close friend of mine because of our ambitions and aspirations to the priesthood.

Yoba could come to my house when I am not there and my mother would serve him with food and drink. I too would go to Yoba's house and eat everything his mother was offering. We were friends and family at the same time. Sometimes friendship is greater than family ties. And we knew all our relationships with our girlfriends.

But the troubling water came in the eve of the state exams that would allow the secondary finalists to go to University. Father was away and mother has little means to feed us. Prior to this particular period, we need to remind people that at the past time 1965-1970, Kinshasa was a natural converted loft: the ecosystem of the North side of Lemba's zone was providing us with important fruits that was taking us full day to spend outside our homes to the point that with the product of cueillette and fisheries and hunting, we would come back home in the evening content to eating our own products of our sweat.

There were fruits like Mbuma liboto, Mbuma makaku, Tondolo, Mbila esobe we used to eat in the savannah of Kinshasa. These alone would leave use with a full stomach forgetting, sometimes, the food our mothers would have cooked. After these seasonal periods came the urbanization that ripped us of the benefits of nature and brought with her the challenging time for many youths. As a result, later on at the eve of the state's exams, with the lack of reserve I had to go write the Examens d'Etat with an empty stomach. The exam would last from eight o'clock in the morning to three o'clock for one to two weeks. In the end Matukimina came up (sadly) with 57 percent, Yoba came up with 61 percent and I came up with 50 percent the passing note, (1983).

If there are exams in the world, the world must know that the state exams in Zaire, in 1970 to 1985 were the most difficult exams in the world. The proof is that during the preparation of these exams, students, country wide, were becoming genius in every field of science. Knowledge and critical thinking were the keys to passing the exam.

Even thought I was given the license to teach with 50% passing notes, I went to the province to became the best teacher in Kwilu-NgoNgo, and because of that I was sent to the Catholic Grand Seminar of philosophy and Theology, MAYIDI, where in the first year I passed with 64 %; then went to Angola, and then to Rome/Italy (1987) were I was getting mostly A+ (9 or 10 by 10) for my exams, then I came to York University in Toronto, Canada where I got my degree in Sociology, and then another degree from the University of Ottawa in Education, and now the Master's Degree in Theology from one of the best Universities in the World, the University of Toronto. The first two Canadians degrees, I studied in the French language but for my Master, I have decided to do that in English.

Based on this great past and this love of knowledge, I became the teacher and the Television Producer and Host who did not put beside my passion for music with 6 Albums CD released. On top of that I am fulfilling the sacred task of being a father of a wonderful Daughter who is doing well academically and socially.

Since we trend, at the end, to recognize that the child is her/his mother, father, even his/her grand-parents in characters, we should also recognize that it is a dilemma to finally assert to whom he/she belongs to if not to him/herself. We, in Africa, do not call a child "It"; we say He or She because we share the conviction and belief that he /she is a human being since conception.

CHAPTER 3
CHILD:

"TO WHOM DOES THE CHILD BELONG" IN ANCIENT, MODERN AND POST MODERN FAMILY

In every country in Africa, Europe and all over the world, family is considered as the basic social unit of society. Consisting of the father, the mother and children. The family represents particularly for children (evidently in a marriage environment), the first educational experience of their life. In short, the child is the: contribution that a man and a woman make to humanity for the achievement of its sole objective existence; the child is the product of the union between the father and the mother.

Many forums are called for people to talk about the child. What it is, what it should be and what it will be. However, we must admit that most of these debates and studies end up in the air. No one has yet succeeded in providing a definition that encompasses all of these questions.

In the Kongo Zone (the Kongo world) since the beginning of time, parents, have consistently and loudly declared: "the child is our blood". This is more so for the father for whom the child is his own blood: "it came out of my back, it is me". This declaration on the part of the father demonstrates generally the power the father has over the child. Most often and above all, this consideration on the part of parents is the basis for parents motivation to give the necessary care that every parent feels obligated to give to the child.

One way or another, any attempt to prove the existence of an alternative to this reality will eventually mean to get out of the family circle or even the clan entirely. The severest sanctions and evil deeds of the ancestors will often follow such an act. The child for the Kongo man is forever followed by parents. Because, even though the child grows into an adult or even becomes mother or father to his or her own children, as long as his father is alive, the child retains title as a child. Thus, among the Kongo, irrespective of the sex or physical condition, a child remains a child forever.

Parents keep a jealous and envious eye on the child. Among all the things that parents provide for the child, each of their little gestures has an objective. This fact supports the statement that parents perform utilitarian acts. For every significant good deed to the child, parents expect a certain return in the near future. These are the kind of statements made by certain parents who experience, disobedience from a child: "Tala nge keba, meso meto kwa nge tu tudidi; tala bonso u ta vangila muana mbuta . . . ma mbote mata vanga mbuta aku nge mpe utu songa kiese ye ngemba". Translation: . . . do not waste, do as others do. Follow the good example, the wise, rich and intelligent child is the source of joy for the parents or again: "Kizolele sala kisalu kia fua ko, konso salu ye Futu andi". Translation: every good deed deserves a good return, the best that can be.

CHAPTER 4
THE CHILD AND MARRIAGE

Marriage is a civil contract, public and solemn by which a man and a woman unite for a specific purpose. Stated briefly, it is an act of union by which two spouses acquire freedom of action and operation.

During past Centuries, Kongo men sought to acquire several wives for purely social and economic reasons. This meant having several wives (for farm labor which kept all of them busy with the major part of the product of their labor owned by the husband who gets very rich through the sweat of his other wives). As time passed, polygamy acquired another connotation. It became the very expression of a human need for which man assumed the responsibility and guilt in case of failure to satisfy the need. To marry several women became a sure method for giving to humanity the maximum number of people needed to accomplish its destiny. However prevalent, polygamy could not stop or destroy monogamy.

In any case, there were still men who preferred to marry one wife for fear of feeling guilty if the education of the children is not properly accomplished. Many more rejected polygamy in the interest of the clan which feared that good blood could be given to other clans. Members of the clan that gave birth to intellectuals and wise men married among themselves. For these clans, to practice polygamy signified if not the pollution of the reputation of the clan, the final acceptance to give opportunities to other clans. This practice was very common among the adepts of ZOROASTRISM who, for fear of falling under the spell of ANGRA MANYU, (religiously considered a bad principle to follow), and in their efforts to avoid becoming slaves to MANYU, their ties to each other degenerated into an obsession for the simple reason to protect the purity of the body and of the spirit. Members of the same family or of the same religion married each other.

In extreme cases, brothers and sisters of the same family slept with each other. (C of HN classes napp, diction Nichtch vistlichen, 499-512). This incestuous relation was common in Africa in the case of LEVIRAT and SORORAT. It is by the way one of the taboos the MUKONGO man respects. The slightest violation of this taboo can cause death. It can be partially pardonable in the case where, innocently, it happened beyond the boarders of the clan. However, even in the latter case, if it happened to the knowledge of the wise men and notables of the clan, it was often the practice to kill the child born out of this relationship and to force the couple to divorce.

With regard to our question as to whom the child belongs, no one has attempted to formulate a complete answer in the opinion of many for the simple reason that confusion still reigns. What is certain is that everything changes from the moment a child is conceived. To think of copulation is a simple idea, perhaps an illusion that becomes a reality later on.

According to Plato the Greek philosopher, we would agree to say that even the idea that we have is not the fruit of our effort. The distinction made by PLATO between two worlds, one of sense and the other of ideas confirms that ideas are an external force. Thus, if ideas that dominate our cognitive life respond to this rule of import-export, how could it not correspond to the relationship of children to their parents?

Fortunately, with regard to this complex subject, Doctor Jean Rostand, a general Practitioner, Paediatrics tells us,: "let us not confuse things, let us remember that from the beginning, the embryo is a distinct organism with its own life. Its genetic code has nothing to do with the maternal cells that surround it. Its heart does not beat at the same rhythm as its mother. Its blood is not necessarily of the same group. In brief, the mother is the hostess of the child, she is not its owner. Moreover the child belongs less to the state. The role of parents is to supervise the child. If they fail in their obligations, the state which is the guardian of human rights, must protect the child.

These few words support the statement that the child is someone other than what we think it is. It would cause great pain to a MUKONGO mother to realize that she is not her child and that her child is not her, especially when she considers this load that she caries since nine months and the madness caused by the confusion, the heat and the anguish of educating the child.

Despite all this, Madame EDIT of Christian Science: tells us and that: "truth must be an uninterrupted activity and not something that happens when we are assailed by the trials of life". In ancient China, a woman that was overwhelmed by concern for this reality (which is the child) went to consult a wise man who spoke in these terms: "your children are not your children. They are the sons and daughters of nature's call to itself. Although they are with you, they do not belong to you; you can give them your love but never your thoughts. You can hold their bodies but not their souls, because their souls live in the house that you cannot visit. Not even in your dreams. You can attempt to be like them, but do not try to make them like you.

Because, life cannot go in reverse nor does it stay with yesterday. You are the Arches with which your children, like living arrows are projected. The Archer sees the target on the way to infinity and exerts strength to ensure that the arrows fly fast and far. Let your force through the arm of the Archer be for joy; because as much as the Archer loves the arrows that fly, the Archer also loves the arch which is stable".

It is reliably evident for us to add this prophesy to the divine reality of Christianity, which does not only exalt paternity as divine, but expands it to include every believer in God (Father Creator of Heaven and earth), as well as every follower of the good news.

Explained in these terms a MUKONGO child must avoid committing the most grievance of all sins which is to dare tell the parents that he or she does not belong to them. The least attempt to do this provokes the anger of parents and could easily cause a lot of other things against the child.

CHAPTER 5
WESTERN PERSPECTIVE

The value of the white child is different from that of the child in Africa for the simple fact that westerners think differently about children. According to those who are familiar with the subject, the white child, from the earliest age, sleeps alone in its own specific bed. Contact between mother and child is limited to moments of care, feeding and other needs. For the nobility, a bank account is opened in the name of the child; and when travelling in a car for leisure or on other occasions, the child's own seat is put separately away from the parents. These few examples in behavior illustrate that parental affection for the child among whites is conditional and different from that of the African mother, who under many conditions and in many circumstances remains closely attached to the child at all times.

In spite all these, we can see that the concept of CHILD has a generally undefined coloration. No living person truly understands whether a child belongs to the parent or not. However, parents must know that it is their obligation to help the child grow into a useful member of society. They must provide the child with the most beneficial know-how and the goods necessary for the child to live a decent life.

Indeed, our conscience will be clear if we accept the fact that the child could not but be itself. The child is not its father, neither its mother nor its uncle. It is someone else; it is what it is, sent by somebody other than its kind. This is evident from our close observation of new families in countries such as Angola, and the Democratic Republic of Congo (formerly Zaire) and certain other countries in Central Africa, where a few months after the marriage of their children, many BOKILOS (in-law) become disenchanted with the behavior of their children and often take them to the KIZONZI (palaver house or native court).

It is sad to see a parent, who, for a moment was joyful at the wedding of the son or daughter, obliged soon after to take back the daughter or niece as a result of being caught cheating with another man; or in the case of the son, returning home before nightfall and before his wife.

Upon analysis of all information, we must ask the question that if indeed the child is its parents, why does it not behave in exactly the same way as they do? In fact, according to the KINOIS (the inhabitants of KINSHASA, the capital City of Congo-Zaire): "BABOTAKA MWANA KASI BABOTAKA MOTEMA TE", translation:—You bear a child but not its heart.

Therefore, parents all over the world, especially those in the Third World, should discard the idea that the child is a breadwinner or a kind of long-term investment. To come to the conclusion that the child that does not behave according to our expectations is a heavy load, is also a serious mistake. Nobody likes to lift a heavy load; and when it is lifted, the bearer is under pressure to put it down. It is entirely left to the child to be conscious of the fact that parents are worth its attention, care and support during their old age.

Yes we might assert and claim that the child is itself neither the father nor the mother but in this matter, conception of a lineage need to be determined by one side of the parent in order to dissipate any dispute in the future of the child. So said so far, our findings lead us to this conclusion.

So, this is our position on the relation between parents and their children. But before us great mind and savvy people like Cheikh Anta Diop had to face this debate and discourse on the Domains of Matriarchy and of Patriarchy in classical Antiquity, which was in fact his Doctorate thesis. When Anta Diop was ready to defend his Thesis on this topic, he was told that he needed to extend his research outside the African sphere. He met the challenge by bringing up to light the experiences of North American previous families by quoting Engels who copied Arthur Wright, the missionary and then Cheikh mentioned the experiences in Europe, finally to conclude with the African experiences. The texts go as follow:

CHAPTER 6
MATRIARCHI AND PATRIARCHY

" . . . Usually, the female portion ruled the house, the stores were in common; but woe to the luckless husband or lover who was too shiftless to do his share of the providing. No matter how many children, or whatever goods he might have in the house, he might at any time be ordered to pick up his blanket and budge; and after such orders it would not be healthy for him to attempt to disobey. The house would be too hot for him; and . . . he must retreat to his own clan (gens); or, as was often done, go and start a new matrimonial alliance in some other. The women were the great power among the clans (gentes), as everywhere else. They did not hesitate, when occasion required, 'to knock off the horns' as it was technically called, from the head of a chief, and send him back to the ranks of the warriors."[14]

We can see two aspects in these customs of the Iroquois people. The ruling of the house by women; the same notion that emanated in Africa and which the Greek people called: Economy Politics, the management of the house which was done by women; and the second aspect is the control of the marriage also directed and instructed by a woman.

Cheikh Anta Diop goes further that if the Indo-European woman in providing the dowry cannot be said to be buying her husband, no more can the African man in providing one be said to purchase his wife.[15] Instead, in parallel with this symbol, we have a life testimony regarding the respect of females; President Mobutu Sese Seko of Zaire, actually known as the Democratic Republic of Congo, regardless of his aggressiveness in character, always called females Mama, meaning

---

[14] Cheickh Anta Diop, *The Cultural Unity of Black Africa: The Domaine of Patriarchy and Matriarchy in Classicalal Antiquity* (London: Karnak House, 1989), 28.

[15] Cheikh Anta Diop, *The Cultural Unity of Black Africa*, 28.

Mother, no matter what age they were. This kind of respect can only be found in Africa, the birthplace of this humanity.

It can equally be understood that descent should be reckoned in these two social structures, from that married partner who does not leave the clan after marriage. With the Indo-European nomad descent will be patrilineal, his wife being only a stranger in his genos; in contrast to this, among sedentary peoples descent will be matrilineal because it is the man who is a stranger, whom the woman can at any moment repudiate if he does not perform all his conjugal duties satisfactorily.

These observations demonstrate that the social rank of the woman and her esteem belong exclusively to the structure of society which allows her to play a leading economic role.

When the husband, said Cheikh Anta Diop, on the other hand, is a stranger, having no family in Ireland, the small family which he found is incorporated into his wife's family: it is called "blue family" (glas-fine), because the husband is considered to have come from across the sea; it is then said that the "marriage" belongs to the man and the "property" to the woman.[16] Moreover, this does not prevent the role of head of the family being filled by man, although it is sometimes occupied by a woman: but among the peoples who do only admit of female consanguinity, the head of the family is the blood brother of the mother. Among other peoples, it is the father . . . [17]

Among Southern societies all that relates to the mother is sacred; her authority is so to speak, unlimited. She can choose, for example, a partner for her own child without previously consulting the interested party. This custom, which is linked with agricultural life, exits likewise among the Iroquois . . . Every society in Black Africa is convinced of the idea that the destiny of a child depends solely on its mother and, in particular, on the labor which the later will provide in the matrimonial home. Thus it is not rare to see women quietly putting up with unfairness on the part of their husbands, from the conviction that the greatest benefit for their children will result from it. It must

---

[16]   Ibid., 29.
[17]   Ibid., 30.

be understood by this that children will be given every opportunity to succeed in any of their undertakings and that they will be spared from 'bad luck' and misfortune of all sorts, that they will be successful and not failures.[18]

Toujours dans le Sud, en Afrique central, le feu Professeur Buakassa dit ceci a propos de LUVILA (le Clan):

> La tradition Kongo compte plusieurs references identitaires, la premiere etant le LUVILA. Si, par exemple, un Kongo va dans un village ou il ne connait personne demander une femme en marriage, la premiere des questions qu'on lui pose n'est pas "qu'est-ce qu'il fait?" mais bien "quell est son LUVILA?". Et s'il arrive qu'on lui pose la question "quell est son son village?" ou "quells sont ses parents?", il a encore-la, sous–entendue, la question "quell est son LUVILA?[19]

Always in the South, in Africa central, the late professor Buakassa said this has purpose of LUVILA (the Clan): "Tradition Kongo relies several self-defining references, the first being LUVILA. If, for instance, a Kongo goes to a village or where he knows nobody to ask a woman for a marriage, the first of the questions which they put down to him is not "what it makes?" but definitely "what is his LUVILA?". And if it happens that they ask him question "what his village is?" or "what are his parents?", it still has her, under-heard, question "what is its LUVILA?"

Le terme LUVILA, qui peut se traduire par le mot clan, designe un espace theorique d'appartenance familiale definie comme entite, une personnalite morale, comprenant des personnes passees, presents et a venir, reliees entre elles par le partage d'une meme vie en ligne de filiation matrilineaire, depuis un ancetre commun situe a l'origine, au commencement, au temps de la foundation de la societe et des clans. Il delimite une zone de vie globale a l'interieur de laquelle il est interdit aux membres y appartenant de se marier entre eux. Il leur fait porter un meme nom propre qui les distingue des personnes appartenant

---

[18] Cheikh Anta Diop, *The Cultural Unity of Black Africa*, 31.

[19] Gerard Buakasa, "Iitineraire d'un Nganga Simoni Makaya Ndonzoau," in 6.

a d'autres TUVILA (plur. De LUVILA) au sein de la communaute ethnique. (P.6 Iitineraire d'un Nganga Simoni Makaya Ndonzoau by Gerard Buakasa).

The term LUVILA, which can be translated by word clan, indicates, a theorical space of family membership defines as entity, a moral personality, consisting of persons in the past, (those who died), presents and has to come, linked between them by the distribution of an online life of the same matrilinear filiation, since a common ancestor locates has origin, in the beginning, at the time of the foundation of society and clans. It delimits a zone of total life as the interior of which it is forbidden members belonging to, to get married between them. It makes them carry the same, proper name which differentiates them of belonging persons has other TUVILA (lineage) or clan.[20]

Therefore, not ignoring the political wrongfulness of the United States of America's constitution on race and belonging, which says that a drop of blood from one of the Black parents makes a child Black; could be challenged in consideration of these numerous examinations. We should then point out and indicate that the children born of a mixed race relationship or marriage who are in a search of identity or belonging, should lean on their mothers lineage instead of claiming in any manners their paternal scale.

From these few lines, we can confirm that descent in family would be or are at first matrilineal. But in order to avoid contradiction and contrast with our previous conclusion, and considering the two most ancient prayers we put here that a child is a God's property, we really need to be careful and vigilant in discerning that during the nine months of pregnancy, the child solely belongs to the mother when he or she comes out, he is a part of the humanity. This is why in Africa we very often say: "It takes a village to raise a child", because the child benefits from everyone's care. But the self-realization of being is partially his /her own and rarely societal. The most important aspect in all of this remains the communication. From the communication with others we can surely obtain our (own) self-realization.

---

[20]   Gerard Buakasa, "Iitineraire d'un Nganga Simoni Makaya Ndonzoau," 6.

While walking around this point about matriarchal; one aspect needs to be remembered; Women used to have a dynamic and significant place in the society; for instant the Instruction of Ptah-Hotep and the Instruction of Ke'Gemni recommend that humanity treats a woman with all due respect and consideration; when it states clearly:

"Again, he 'knows nothing' of duties to the mother, although he is so insistent on duties to the father; but the high position of women and their matriarchal privileges oppose any deduction that Egyptian manners were somewhat to seek in this direction." It continued to say that a man is a grief to his mother, Eney of the 12th Dynasty (B.C. 2700) Said to his Son:

> I gave thee thy mother, she that bore thee with much suffering . . .
> She placed thee at the Chamber of Instruction for the sake
> of thine instruction in books; she was constant to thee daily,
> having loaves and beer in her house. When thou art grown, and
> hast taken to thee a wife, being master in thy house, cast thine
> eyes on the one that gave thee birth and provided thee with all
> good things, as did thy mother. Let her not reproach thee, lest
> she lift up her hands to the God, and He hear her prayer."[21]

This notion of respect vis-à-vis women transcends time; it was the jealousy and the bad faith of Indo-Europeans men that were fed-up with the high social rank of women to the point that they lowered the status of woman. Her supremacy was seen as an obstacle to the men's ascent from the social failure and their weak misplaced competitive endeavor in many matters.

Many would think that a woman is the one who brings curse to the man, while we know for sure that the true story about Adam (which was also a legend scripted in the walls of Egypt) Adam was struggling with many issues in his life (after failing from his first marriage with LILITH his first wife), and as a consequence, he asked (prayed) God for Wisdom, and God sent him Eve, a woman, a wife as wisdom. But time has perpetuated the evil intention of the Indo-Europeans men that sees a woman as a feable and weak being. In reality, we all belong to

---

[21]   *The Instruction of Ptah-Hotep and the Instruction of Ke'Gemni*, 33.

women's care even thought we men can (may be) physically, pretend to be the highest achievers. The most degrading thing, humanly speaking, is the fact that the Europeans who wrote the So-called Sacred book, the Bible, encouraged activities such as incest,1 Corinthians 7 verses 36-38. This Saint Paul's vision, a vision of the Indo-Europeans, is intended not just for their own style of life, but mostly and predominantly to mislead the culture of values which is the African Culture.

In order for us to see clearly, we need to rely on the writings of Ivan Van Sertima and friends, in the book called **"Black Women in Antiquity"**, in which conclusion, Sertima argues: "In spite of this perennial contest with, and occasional or perpetual suppression by, the male, her role in the history and development of civilization has been just as great. To prove this is not easy since a great deal of history would have to be rewritten with a different emphasis and orientation."[22]

What really triggered this conclusion is the examination of the preceding, "In an earlier preparation for this special volume, **Black Women in Antiquity**, we were tempted to dwell upon the controversy raging over the first woman, our earliest known human ancestor, the African mother of all mankind, "Lucy.", three and half million years, ago, three feet, sixty pounds, and her place of origin (Ethiopia). Andromeda, daughter of the Ethiopian king, Cepheus, is taken to wife by the legendary Greek hero, Perseus. Circe the magician and enchantress of Homer's Odyssey, is painted on Grecian vases, as a black woman. Her niece, Medea, daughter of the Colchian king, Aeetes, uses her powers to help young Jason in his quest for the golden fleece. Larry Williams and Charles Finc trace these women, so prominent in Greek myth, back to their Ethiopian origins.

They also introduce us to the most powerful line of all black queens—the Candaces (from the Meroitic "Kentake", which means Queen-Mother). They point out that unlike Egyptian Queens, who largely owed their authority to being the great wives of pharaohs (Hatshepsut being the exception), Ethiopian Queens were independent rulers. This raises the

---

[22]   Ivan Van Sertima, *Black Women in Antiquity* (New Brunswick- U.S.A: Library of Congress, 1984), 1-11.

question as to what extent early African matriarchal patterns underwent changes as Africans moved down northwards into Egypt. Williams and Finch contend, however, that "such independent female rulers are found throughout Africa in time and space" and that "the relative frequency of the queenship compared to other parts of the world—reflected the persistent matriarchal patterns in Africa through the course of history."[23]

The period of Ethiopian history covered by these researchers encompasses about two thousands years (from 1000 B.C. to 1000 A.D.). Barring Candaces in the much later Meroitic period, no black queen of ancient times (or no queen for that matter) had such a legend built around her as Makeda, the queen of Sheba. She is known in the Bible as the great black beauty who melted King Solomon's heart into a song. The child she bore for him, Menelik, started the Solomonid line of Ethiopian kings, a line which, but for an interruption of 300 years, continued right down to the late Haile Selassie.

Williams and Finch show that the story of the romance between Solomon and the queen of Sheba probably overshadows more important roles and accomplishments of this black queen. She organized an extensive trade network and ruled an empire larger and more substantial than Solomon's. Her business with him involving commercial and diplomatic settlements, not just romantic concerns. The hospitality he lavished upon her was a tribute not simply to her beauty but to her position of eminence and influence in the ancient world . . . These queens (Candaces, Amanirenas and others), were not only masters of the states, but masters of the spiritual capitals as well. According to Diedre Wimby, the man was the personification of divine authority, the woman the source of his power. The queen was the guardian of the royal lineage. The power of the mother or wife in the royal house of Kemet did often balance out that of the pharaoh, even in cases where she was not reigning.

Sonia Sanchez contrast the African myth of Osiris and Isis against the patriarchal myth of Adam and Eve. The woman in Africa was not seen as a rib or appendage of afterthought to man, but as his divine equal. "The goddesses retained their prestige in becoming wives: the couple was the religious and social unit; woman seemed to be allied with and

---

[23]   Ivan Van Sertima, *Black Women in Antiquity*, 5-6.

complementary to man: woman has the same rights as man, the same powers in court: she inherited, she owned property." . . . And following the strongest African custom, strengthened by a Nubian in the royal bed, it is the princesses, not the princes, who enjoy venerated status. The importance of the female in the royal family is stressed.

Another queen of the south but a mythical one, among the firstborn of the goddesses, is Isis. Eloise McKinney-Johnson presents her as Egypt's quintessential sweetheart, wife, and mother. She is worshipped as the sister-wife of Osiris, the "King of the Dead," and mother of Horus, the "King of the Living." Egypt, Greece, and Rome bowed down to this black African goddess. In one of his conferences, professor Sertima pointed out that all the white kings of Europe got married to the black African wives, regardless of their marital status.[24]

Runoko Rashidi also touches on this aspect of Isis as the original black Madonna. Statues of her and the baby Horus, whom she suckles, passed for representations of Mary and Jesus in many European churches, especially those in Italy (the first Euro-Christian shrines). In his erudite essay on the three African goddesses who exerted the largest influence in ancient times, Rashidi gives us the historical background to the cults that grew up around them, not only in Africa but in Greece, in Rome, in Minoan Crete, in Phoenicia, in parts of Asia, even (in some instances) in the British Isles. There is Hathor, the self-begetting goddess, donor of life, protector of the dead, goddess too of the senses, linked with laughter and dance and song and music. The religious concepts behind these African goddesses lie not in the Nile Valley (although the most substantial documentation of them may be found there) but in the Great Lakes region of East/Central Africa. There, "in the continental heartland, the primordial center, occurred the molding and forming of the religious and philosophical ideas that were to critically shape the world."

Ivan Van Sertima did not tarnish the information in the conclusion of his introduction of Black Women in Antiquity. He wrote, according to the essay by the historian Edward Scobie, which deals with black woman in early Europe; she (black woman), occupies extreme positions in European

---

[24] Ivan Van Sertima, *Black Women in Antiquity,* 8-9.

imagination. She is on the one hand the sex goddess and courtesan. The Kings and the noblemen of France and Portugal, a cardinal in Italy, later to become pope, Baudelaire and Shakespeare, greatest of poets, rush to her bed. She is so irresistible that, in spite of all the racial prejudices of the day, her blood ultimately runs through the royal and noble families of Europe—Queen Charlotte Sophie, the Duke of Florence, the Medicis, the Gonzagas, the Duchess of Alafoes, St. Hilaire, son of Louis XV—the list is great. Artemis, the Greek goddess of chastity is black; she is wise. Minerva, the goddess of wisdom was an African princess; she is a saint, as are the black Madonna of Loretta in Italy, Nuria in Spain, Czestochowa in Poland.

Woman has lived under the shadow of man's ego, even as, in the past few centuries, the black has lived under the shadow of the white. The myth of female inferiority seems to have been far more developed in Europe and Asia than in Africa . . . . in Africa, regardless of the countervailing myths, like that of Isis and Osiris, which ranked woman as a divine equal. Women complemented, but they also competed with men, even, at times, embracing both male and female attributes and appurtenances (as was the case with Hatshepsut and Nzinga) in order to establish her domination.[25]

On the top of all of the lies from Indo-Europeans, the most desgasting of all: Jeanne D'Arc. Joan of Ark.

> Ces nouvelles pages me rappellent un cure, encore pas trop vieux, docteur en theologie et chercheur d'insolite, qui avait travaille pendant plus d'une dizaine d'annees sur Jeanne d'Arc, la francaise. A deux reprises, il a annonce publiquement (et c'est une erreur) la prochaine publication des resultats surprenants de ses decouvertes non conformes a la << verite >> historique. Il a d'abord explique des labyrintes genealogiques, des inexactitudes de faits, des contradictions, la presence de plusieurs evenements caches . . . etc . . . Il a precise que la realite vecue par Jeanne d'Arc ne correspond pas a l'image fabriquee par la version officielle de l'histoire (non approfondie, laissant subsister de grandes places d'ombres incomprehensibles) . . .

---

[25]   Ivan Van Sertima, *Black Women in Antiquity*, 1-11.

. . . Des voyantes et mediums de tous genres se sont saisis ou ont ete saisis par ce phenomene et se sont sentis revivre dans le corps meme de cette Jeanne d'Arc insaisissable et mysterieuse, mais brulee ou l'evadee . . . Plus recemment, une dame, avec qui j'ai eu l'occasion d'etudier l'Histoire des idees religieuses, dans une Universite du sud de la France, m'a rapporte des recits detailles allant dans le sens d'un truquage complet du proces et d'un changement de corps juste avant le moment du bucher . . . La vraie Jeanne d'Arc n'avait pas ete brulee . . . La transformation des donnees etait trop invraisemblable et trop compliquee pour pouvoir etre efficace . . . Double voie, donc, concernant Jeanne et, sur l'une et sur l'autre, du Mysterieux, une convergence remarquable de l'heroique et de l'inspiration. Comme dans tout evenement important, quelque chose reste voile, volontairement ou non, quelque chose est inconnaissable et quelque chose est exprime, manifeste, apparent . . . L'implicite qui chemine, malgre les aleas de l'empirique et qui est fondateur radical du sens dit, n'a pas a etre dilapide. Mais, quelques indications peuvent etre simplement suggerees et laissees a la liberte de comprehension de chacune et de chacun, dit le Professeur Henri Louis Canal.[26]

Le proces de Jeanne d'Arc a ete truque;

Jeanne d'Arc Hierophore;

Shortly, the story of Joan of Ark was a cover up; let's say a falsification of history. She was not burned alive. The authorities substituted her with another woman. Also, the genealogy of Joan of Ark is absurd; the person who wrote a book to reveal the truth about her was killed, or even buried alive according to some accounts.

People should ask themselves why the president of the tribunal went alone to see the captive after everybody else left? Why victim's face was dissimulated and covered to the public?

Why after one hour, final sentence was not pronounced and execution

---

[26] Rudy Mbemba dia BENAZO-MBANZULU, *Le Proces de KIMPA VITA la Jeanne d'Arc Congolaise* (Paris: L'harmattan, 2002), 5-14.

was put in hurry in the absence of officials? Why the stake (woodshed) was so voluminous compare to others? Why the register of the office of the Bishop of Rouen does not mention any stake (fire) for the death of Joan of Ark?

Many answers need to be provided, otherwise, we stick to our truth. You can tell this is the kind of perpetual Mis-Education Charles H. Wesley and Thelma D. Perry are talking about in the introduction of Carter G. Woodson's book, "Mis-Education of the Negro", when they said:

"Mis-Education criticizes the system, and explains the vicious circle that results from mis-educated individuals graduating, then proceeding to teach and mis-educate others."[27]

To understand the magnitude of the situation, ask yourself, how many of these fallacious stories are out there and for how long have they been teaching them and to whom?

Now that we have enlightened our minds and spirits with the benefits of our biological Fathers and Mothers, on the side, we also must, as any becoming man or woman, have a Spiritual Father or Mother from whom we also learn. For me, my father played both roles but because he, as my father, venerates Ntumua Kimbangu, I also automatically embraced Ntumua Kimbangu (who is well known by European and American elites more than Kongolese and Africans), as my Spiritual Father and we are going to reveal the Black envoy of God through other friends who have met or studied Him; but before we go there, let's inform the readers about Ntumua Kimbangu's wonders:

<u>Before outlining some of the wonders of Ntumua Kimbangu, we invite and urge the world to consult the writing testimonies of the American Baptist Pastor Jennings (in the Library of Congress in the U.S.A.) and the testimonies of the Royal family of Belgium on Kimbangu.</u>

---

[27]   Carter G. Woodson and Willie Lynch, *The Mis-Education of the Negro and the Willie Lynch letter* (Washington, D.C: MAISON D'EDITION,.1933), 6.

CHAPTER 7
SPIRITUAL FATHER/MOTHER

Ntumua Kimbangu [28]

- healed the woman who was very sick in the village close to Nkamba;
- Arrested a dozen of sorcerers in the nearby village (all of them were naked);
- He resurrected a child by the name of Dina;
- He resurrected and brought to life 146 dead;
- He healed a multitude of people coming from the three Congo (Angola, Belgian Congo and French Congo); and hospitals became emptied;
- A soldier who took His Nzombo (kind of fish in the Congo, a fish that lives in the water but can claimb the palm tree to go look for food), after, eating that fish, everything that soldier eat, tasted like a Nzombo (fish);
- He asked Mpungu Tulendo that He takes Him to go preach around Congo and it was granted; when the Belgians arrested Him, they wanted to take Him to the North Eastern part of Congo by Airplane, the plane could not fly; they then took the boat through the Congo River and every village where the colonials stopped and put Ntumua Kimbangu in a Prison, He planted a spiritual seed all along the way;
- While in prison, He will come out (freed Himself and left Prison while the door of His cell was closed), He would appear to people

---

[28] The following texts are taken from Interviews and the International Conference on Simon Kimbangu organized by the Kimbanguits. Permission was granted to any one willing to write and publish the book. Everything was said in Lingala and French; this translation is mine. The term Ntumua means Envoy.

and preach them, sometimes at 4 O'Clock in the morning, sometimes at ten o'clock in the night;

- He does not matter how hard they enchained Him, He always come out of the chains;
- He healed a blind man while in Prison;
- He appeared on the top of the flag tree in Lowa (Kisangani);
- On the day of and During His arrest, He doubled Himself and took His children, while Belgians police where beating Him, and brought the children to the forest of the village of Ndemba N'Kenge to a secure place; His children could see that Father was been beaten;
- The Colonial Belgians flag and the picture of the king felt down and were scattered in two pieces while the military court was judging Him=Ntumua Kimbangu;
- He, on the demand of the Belgians leaders, went (without airplane) to Europe to free the Belgians King that was imprisoned by the Germans;
- On a special occasion, Belgians arrested Him in Europe and brought Him back to Congo-Kinshasa via brazza-ville as a white man and while He still was in prison; and when He landed in Congo, He became a Black man, Belgians called the authorities in Lubumbashi (Lubumba Nsi) where He was in prison to asked if He was there, the authorities confirmed He was over there in prison because they could see Him, they even verified the body sign He beard on the neck and He was the same person;
- He made a rain of money falls down in Mbanza Ngungu; after the Belgians authorities asked Him if He has money to form a Church. First, He told them, my money is my people, and because the Belgians insisted on the question, He put His both hands into His pockets sides and when lifted them up, a rain of money started to fall down in the entire surrounding region of Mbanza Ngungu;
- On many occasions they shot at Him, bullets became water;
- They put Him in the closed hot oil, fuel barrel and dumped it in the Congo River in Lutendele, the Spirits of water could not retain Him, He came out and the Belgians and Congoleses saw

him on the top of the barrel; after that He again gave Himself to the Belgians authorities;

- He told people He will die on a particular Friday (October 12th, 1951) at 3 O'clock and it happened as He said (one eye closed, one opened);
- The Belgian doctor performed the autopsy on Kimbangu's body and could not find any vital organs, he panicked and run away;
- Three days after, He came back to life, He resurrected in a figure of a soldier reading His sacred Book on the road—the Belgian colonial soldier who saw Him that Sunday at 5:00 a.m. reading His book on the road, stopped Kimbangu and took the book by force and the soldier's hands became multiplied by ten, he became afraid and dropped the book and run away;
- Kimbangu appeared in Hotel Regina in Kinshasa where Belgian Colonials were celebrating and Belgians panicked and the celebration ended;
- His family and many people saw Him alive and they still see Him to these days all around Congo;
- To their way from Lufutoto to Mbanza Ngungu, when His disciples were wondering about the night coming because they have to walk, Kimbangu stop the time; 5 p.m. took longer then usual and they arrived within the day light;
- While in Prison in Lubumbashi, a Belgian Catholic priest who was working in the Congo approached Kimbangu for a conversation; Kimbangu asked the Belgian to touch Him on the belt side of His cloth and to hold on, the Belgian priest was transported by Kimbangu for what is known today as the timeless traveling around the world, through which Kimbangu showed that priest Europe and the Vatican in less than five minutes; after this mystic trip, based on what the Belgian priest saw, he quits priesthood, returned to Europe and got married.
- Early in the morning on the day of His resurrection, a Belgian soldier on a motorcycle saw a black soldier on the street reading Ntumua Kimbangu's Holy Book (Fuku kia Zaya), the Captain stopped and grabbed the book, his hands became multiplied (ten

times), and he dropped the book Kimbangu who appeared as a soldier took back the book and disappeared;

– He predicted all the presidents of Congo, including their characters;

– He changed one Belgians who slammed Him to Black and White, after He told that soldier to stop;

– He manifested Himself (alive) to many people including to Papa Mpadi and Papa Diangienda Kuntima (His Son) when He was very young at the Catholic school in Boma where the Belgians took the two sons (First and Last), the second was left in Nkamba with his mother Mama Muilu, the wife of Ntumua Kimbangu;

– He revealed the Mandombe system of writing (scriptures) to the late David Wabeladio;

– He spoke through Mangongele, the savvy young preacher who came with and taught many science formulas to university students as well as to university professors and searchers;

– A Belgian priest was about to poison Ntumua Kimbangu, he prepared (cooked) a pigeon and gave it to Kimbangu, Ntumua Kimbangu asked Him what did you put in this food? To show His power to the Belgian priest, Kimbangu ordered the pigeon to come alive, the pigeon recovered became alive and flied;

– Kimbangu was seen in seven different locations at the same time;

– A Belgian Colonel (in Ndolo prison in Kinshasa), who told Kimbangu that he will send Him back to the prison in Lumbumbashi at seven O'clock in the morning the next day, after He appeared in Kinshasa, Kimbangu told Him if I wanted, you the colonel, you would return as well back to the country of your ancestors tomorrow at 7 a.m.; the next day while Kimbangu was heading back to prison, the Belgians of Kinshasa have found that that Colonel was dead in his bed and they sent his cadavre back to Belgium;

– Kimbangu told the Congoleses and the Africans in 1921 that they will become Independent countries and it happened;

– Kimbangu's prophecy at Mbanza Nsanda is still happening;

– Kimbangu exited the jail cell while the door was still locked; when asked on that 4th day of October 1951, He told the Belgians authorities that His prison time has come to a term;

- Kimbangu told everybody that He will die on Friday October 12, 1951 at 3 O'Clock in the evening and it happened like He said;
- Kimbangu is still appearing to people in the Congo as well as around the world.
- Ntumua Kimbangu did many others wonders we did not mention here;
- Kimbangu was taken to the cemetery in Mbanza Ngungu by the Europeans where He was asked to resurrect dead people if He has power, He did bring back dead people to life but they came back in chains on necks and arms (beware the Church you belong to); the second time Kimbangu was taken to an old cemetery in ruin in Kinshasa (where later on they built La Voix du Zaire, the TV and Radio Station); there Kimbangu resurrected a very young lady who was buried there very longtime ago;
- A Kimbanguist delegation was invited to Rome/Italy by the late Pope John Paul II who told the delegation (which is diminishing for a large number of Congolese) that Kimbangu was one of the Apostles based on everything He has done. Similar declaration was made on my television program by l'Abbe Ngimbi Nseka, who was at that time Rector of the Catholic University of Kinshasa that Kimbangu and Kimpa Vita were considered as the Fathers/Mothers of the Catholic Church.

CHAPTER 8
KIMBANGU ACCORDING TO
PROPHET MANGONGELE

. . . 1500; 1501; 1502; 1503; (502th Anniversary) . . . On the 17th day of December, 1663. The woman who became the Queen of Matamba did remind people that Grand Mother Nzinga has left a three of value that brings out the truth. It name is: NSANDA DIA KONGO.

It is found in the North part of Angola, and in Mbanza Nsanda (in the Democratic Republic of Congo) and in Matadi Mayo near Kinshasa. Her words have revealed the stone we call NTADI DIA KONGO; which we know today as Diamond.

She made appear the copper we wear on our arms. The person who made and polished this copper is MPANZU DIA KONGO. Our ancestors used to wear these copper on their arms and also if you are ready to get married you would need to wear it. Our Ancestors were doing these things in the hope of building a perfect world without sins; where not evil was to be found. But soon as we gave up with our authentic names to adopt different names, from 1500 to this day, 502 anniversary, it came in remembrance of Mama Nzinga on 17th day of December 1763, Kongo's name could not be changed. The name supposed to remain the same.

The one who would remove or change the name Kongo, would pay by having in his/her door, especially in the Kongo river, an animal spirit by the name Mbengu Mbengu. This spiritual animal will be put between Matadi and Boma. Boat cannot go where Mbengu Mbengu is located. In the hardness of our thoughts, by changing the name Kongo, if a stranger or a national come, in order to pass, one needs to show respect of the ancestral ways in order to proceed in peace. This is how we ended up having Mbengu Mbengu. You need to do something, just respect Mbengu by respecting ancestral consigns.

Mbengu Mbengu lives in the water of Congo River in the state of vengeance and it is Mbengu that fills the rivers in the Congo (Matadi-Boma). Its influences are described over the swirling of 33 falls from Kinsuka to Boma. If you do not follow ancestrals consigns, your boat would run over and flop over. Mbengu Mbengu is there to remind the greatness of Kongo through Mama Nzinga since the 17th day of December 1663. As Mama Nzinga told, she fought for 26 years, so remember the name Kongo and the tree of the truth to bring back honors. I was among you in physical form for 87 years and I left power to my great sons and daughters, your ancestors. That is why 502 anniversary needs to be celebrated. Our fashion is not sorcery, because the ancestors were not sorcerers. It is vernacular culture our outfit recognized by UNESCO. Ancestors still live and allow us to live today.

Also, we name everybody elder because when a woman gave birth today, she does not name her child right away but the mother of that woman will call the newborn NKOKO, ancestor or elder (grandson or grand daughter). That is why we call each other Nkoko (ancestor or elder). Before you bear a name, you were called Nkoko. Our generation since 1960 to this day, our fathers struggled to obtain independence, four years later, I was born. When I was born, there was no place of attraction, so, the idea came to my mind to create a city called Batara, city of the messengers of God, created on 15th day of February 2003. We did everything to plant and to growth 19 millions trees. To start, I launched a campaign of collecting grain of fruits people were throwing everywhere in the north of Kinshasa, people called me crazy. Today the result has produced 19 millions trees of fruits. Beside trees, we also have psy-culture for fishes and we plant more.

In 2006, God willing we will reap 5 tons of corn. My idea, when people say Congo is rich, my idea is to take resources, fabricate and then invent from our minerals. And we can put to work at least 175 thousands people into different companies because I do have 444 directions that help me to take care of 20 thousands young people I have here. We do not get loans from any sources, the only thing we have is the wisdom our God has given to our ancestors. We work hard to produce and to finally sell the merchandizes cheaper to our mothers (the population). We want the price to go down in the market. We are not poor we are a rich Kongo. Kongo is rich, from the assembly line of cornflower, rice, manioc, beans, products of rivers, everything our ancestors planted, we are planting them. To my recollection, our generation needs to invent and to create in order to acquire manufacturing companies and fabrics that will benefit us. Work more than Hong Kong that was almost non-existent in 1959, but has become one of the best countries today because of their hard work. God can enlighten you to teach others how to perform at the national level that is why we have produced a lot of good and service.

Coming to raffia, peko in our language; it tree produces palm drink Sese, all of this is produced by mama Nzinga who also named sanza (moon), she is the one who taught all Kongolese woman by telling them that if you want your children to grow up smart and wise, you need to drink at least one glass of nsamba (palm drink) while breast feeding, by doing so, the children will grow with a great brain full of god's wisdom. That was the first pill. But because Europeans could not make a pill based on palm tree drink, they limited their knowledge. Yet palm tree drink procures wisdom.

CHAPTER 9
CREATION

Clothes came from raffia (peko), the ram that produces raffia that is made smooth, with the skin of Mbembe by the machine of mbanzi, the SeSe tree will produce raffia. If the government would like to revive the ancestor's spirit, we will guarantee that tree and make clothes.

About human, we came from our ancestors. God has created us from the fruit called cola-nut that was promised longtime ago. If I created blacks from cola nut, said God, they will protect and nourish the forest, they will sit with gorilla, so to say, our ancestors were made from (makasu) cola-nut. During the time of God's conception, He saw that He has created animals, but animals were fighting; no one could come with the idea of growing foods. Animal does not call its offspring by name; does not make fire; does not prepare a sleeping place; animals are full of disorder by lack of knowledge.

So, God examined His creatures, and looked at the creature that releases odor when it is mature; God then sent a wind that blows on its creatures, especially on Makasu, Heart like, cola-nut with red color like blood; God took Makasu and came to lake Tanganika. (If you hear today Europeans saying that the first oldest bone was collected in Tanzania or Kenya its not true, simply because the explorers were English that is why they attributed the discovery to the English colonies). Black people were made on Kalemi zone, on Nirangongo, in the country of seven volcanoes (Kongo). To these days, if there is war in the Eastern part of Congo it is because Europeans are still following the traces where the first black people came from. That version of history is not taught in schools.[29] When God seized Makasu, and launched the wind that

---

[29] It is in that same region of Kongo Katiopa that ISHANGO Bone was found 20,000 years before the rise of Egypt. ISHANGO BONE is the first calculator or mathematic tool used by the Kongolese in the place where Civilization started earliest on, "near Lake Albert," in Central Africa.

hurts makasu and propulse it to the animal Tanganika which we also called Ngando (crocodile) that kicked Makasu in the water and the man appeared.

God took the second Makasu and hit the crocodile with the words: Nkela oyo akolamba mpe akobimisa solo ya biloko nayo. = create the one who will prepare, who will degage odour of my food. Makasu –cola nut, went to the deep water and emerged as a woman. God took both of them from the water and gave them Cola-nut and the tree He loved most, Mungulu, which we call today, Tabac. Tabac is therefore the First God's tree. Animal does not eat it. It reveals good and evil. If by accident, an animal ended up eating it, that animal will be open to the secrets of the world. And even when a man eats it, he will access good and evil powers. Tabac was not intended for human to smoke it.

Once Tabac is grown, God, will take it to the cave. When He goes to the mountain, He will find it, but not in the forest. Mongulu favorite tree of God was not to be smoked. It serves one purpose: when the Sun rises, thunder or lighting hit it, Mongulu (Tabac) produces fire. Two kind of fire, hidden fire; the one we make and God's fire Kake (thunder or lightning). When God's fire hits Tabac, the odour comes out and fire erupts and after sometimes, vegetables will grow in big quantity and those plantes are sacred. When Europeans in cite Livingstone and Stanley came to the city-village of Botembo, always in the Eastern part of Congo, (beside Diego Cao who came for another mission), the two preceding came in search of ancestral customs and values. They went to Bukavu to get the knowledge and the information about the age of the seven volcanoes in order to possess the City of Ituri.

So, when the two men (Livingstone and Stanley) discovered that a burned Mungulu (Tabac) was producing many goods, they used it to practice magic. Now a white magician who wants to do some tricks, would smoke and blow smoke to do things. Everything was African and mostly Congolese. I remember, in the Kongo sphere, many young people who suffered head diseases and sickness, were cured by a gueriseur (traditional Healer) in a ceremony that consists of blowing smoke over the head of the sick person.[30] God has given us Makasu to prolong life.

---

[30]   What similarity when you observe the Indians (Natives) of America cleansing

To create a bridge between God and the living, just eat or chew Makasu; let one woman sprinkle palm drink, then Mungulu will be placed on top of the fire, to be burned, when the smoke goes up, God is honored and sacred mission can be performed. From that action, all that the good human mind would need or ask would be granted.

On the 03rd day of October 1921, Ntumua Kimbangu promised to send the children of promise; we can see that one young Congolese made a spatial engine with the formula coming from Mangongele. Today we are following those words to find out where Blacks are from, their Gods and what they are to create.

Kimbangu did heal 17,852 sick people and resurrected 146 dead. Before knowing Kimbangu, we need to know Jean Jacques Charles (Diego Cao = God of Dogs) time. He was the Pope's envoy sent by one of his Cardinals, to go to Kongo Kingdom for discovery. So, Diego entered Africa through Mbanza Kongo, the Capital of Kongo Kingdom, there to meet the 5th King of Kongo, Nzinga Nkuvu. This was about 1491— for the 217th Pope Leon X. He asked: Do you know Kimbangu that was promised for today, tomorrow and forever? The answer was simple: Kimbangu who was promised by the Ancestors is already here to free us from the bondage of slavery. To prepare us for new intelligence of mineral resources.

So, in 1491, on May 05th, the Europeans knew Kimbangu without seing Him. Following the genealogy, King Nzinga from Matamba village, the same who gave the name Kongo before the 3rd Century, this Kongolese Queen prophesized that Kimbangu will come. Then we saw Yaya Kimpa Vita from Kianfu village restoring Mbanza Kongo and doing many wonders. At Her time, they saw a big storm and rain with thunders and tree falling, on a Thursday, June 29, the cloud came down to earth and Kimbangu came to this world through the cloud. Because elders of the village knew the times of wonders, they called upon the young lady who did not knew men; Kimpa Vita Isipa.

These village elders told Her that in the forest under the rain, an infant was there, so she chose to go over there take the infant and procure

themselves with smoke.

Him all necessary care. Yaya Kimpa Vita went and took the child and brought Him to the elders of the Village, who told Her, from today on, you are the mother of this child; take care of Him, as promised by our Ancestors. This is the child who used to come to our Ancestors' dreams, He is the one who will save us. Go behind the houses, you will see Egobe.

When white people heard the news, Mr Jean Jacques Charles, Lawrent de Luc, Bernard de Gaulle, on Thursday June 29, 1706, they arrested the young lady under the rain. From the afternoon of that day to Sunday, the white people gave the order to black people to look for wood, around 12 p.m. They took Kimpa Vita to jail while villagers were looking for dry woods, (these Europeans had walked Vita, hands tied from Mbanza Kongo to the mount of Evululu in Kwilu Ngongo). It is the equivalent of walking from Buffalo-New York to Toronto-Canada). At the end of the rain, the stake was set and Kimpa Vita, the Baby and the Soldier of the King were burned alive. Her dust was burned for the second time and then put in container (big Bottle) and taken to the Vatican.

This symbolized the mile stone of the Capuchin Priests in the Kongo Kingdom and the beginning of forced slavery where a human being was taken from Africa just to be sold for $ 260 in Marseille, France before they would be sent to la Fahette, Manhattan in New York, South Carolina, Louisiana, Florida, Cuba, Haitie, Bolivia, Colombia, Venezuela and Brazil. For Africa, it was also the beginning of pure colonization. So, for the first time, Kimbangu was seen there. Honestly, not trial took place in the killing of Kimpa Vita. And there is a need here to say that the practice (of burning someone alive) was properly European, from the Medieval times. Africans burn things but not humans. This is the lieu where Kongolese lost their common memory. After four days of the fire at the stake, on the fifth day, fire was transformed into something unseen. Europeans and the Kongolese, could see Kimpa Vita and the Baby in the full moon walking forward and backward. These traverses were happening to show God's power and resistance.

One account says that while Kimpa Vita and the Baby were burning, a dove came out from the fire and flew to the Northern part of Kongo Kingdom. Still to show Almighty's resistance, from 1706 to 1881, one particular day in 1881, heavy rain fell down in the Northern part, the actual Zaire. Again older people called Papa Kuyela and Mama Makiese Luezi, Papa Kuyela was then called by Ancestors, Kuyela Nzazi, Lukalakala Mbele Nzazi, to go over there and take the young boy who is there alone in the rain; take Him, He is wearing white clothes, He is under the rain and thunders are rolling. He went there in the forest and saw the young-man. Papa Kuyela asked the boy: Who are you? Kimbangu's mouth could not open. Who are you and where do you come from? He asked again. At the same moment, the thunder struck and the young boy answered: My name is Kimbangu. He took the boy to the village; but after that by being afraid, he took Him to Ngombe Kinsuka, to the protestant missionaries. Papa Kuyela told the protestants, this child I took in the forest under the rain, told me His name is Kimbangu. Look after Him. He then was baptized in Ntumba River under the name Simon/ Simoni or Simeon Kimbangu.

When the curse came, things started going terribly wrong, White people betrayed Kimbangu through the Gospel even though He entered their teaching under catechism. Soon Kimbangu's teachings became oriented towards Ancestral benefits. His teachings were as a discovery of black people's awakening, were giving Ancestral wisdom to blacks. White protestant missionaries became furious and mad to the point that they decided to kick Kimbangu out of their circle. He left the protestant mission where papa Kuyela took Him, and went to live (alone) in Mbanza Nsanda, a village in Kimpakasa, living alone without Father, without Mother nor uncle, He really was there alone without a child or wife. Then the new arrival, another wave of white people in the person of Cameron, Kimbangu's mission started. He started healing people, He cured mama Kinzembo, and this one took Kimbangu to Nkamba Village.

From there, Kimbangu met papa Kupenda Kapata who already had his descent family. If you asked the elders of Kimbanguist Churche, their narrative would tell you that Mama Muilu was given to Kimbangu as His wife after His Uncle died. So, Kimbangu married the former wife of His uncle. Kimbangu left Nkamba and came to Kinshasa (Leopold Ville) to work in PLZ and was living in Dodoma. The house where He used to live is now surrounded by crazy people but the Elders of the Churche have built a wall (Brick fence) and the door locked with a safety lock, so no one can enter in. When Kimbangu left Kinshasa for Matadi Kibala, no one knew that was Kimbangu.

At that city, Matadi Mayo is the place where Kimbangu's mission started. Matadi Kibala or Matadi Mayo is the first Centre we know since 1717 where 65 Black Congolese Prophets disappeared from the cages they were put into by Europeans in the preparation of a long deportation trip to Europe where the Europeans priests thought by taking them over there they will finally reveal the Sacred Power of Africans. They were 32 Females and 33 Males. Before the trip to Europe, they were taken from Kimuenza Canal by 45 white Cappucins. When the 65 Prophets knew that they had been taken captives for a far away destination, they started singing spiritual songs and suddenly disappeared. The cages were left empty. Now when Kimbangu arrived there in Matadi Mayo, the Mpeve Kia Kongo (The Spirit of Kongo) surrounded Him and He became invested in Him. Kimbangu started without fear preaching very loud and saying this land is our. It belongs to black people. That was the beginning of Kimbangu's mission.

Kimbangu was not operating in hiding; He was speaking publically without fear. He spoke by the power of African Ancestors. He was already claiming victory over the force of darkness (Whites). Congolese lived and are still living under total ignorance that is why some of them do not know the Creator's envoy, Kimbangu. Knowing Kimbangu is the Truth. (One Congolese was in Belgium defending his Doctorate thesis and called Kimbangu the Prophet. All the white Belgian elders in the hall were outrageous and stopped the young Congolese by telling him that Kimbangu was not a prophet, He was the Envoy of Almighty Himself, NTUMUA. (This is the answer Kimbangu gave the military tribunal that was interrogating Him in Mbanza Ngungu).

This how He identified Himself in front of the Military Tribunal that judged and sentenced Him for life in prison). Since the world began, no one has suffered like Kimbangu. By the same token, no one has accomplished wonders like He did. Not miracles, only wonders. The first wonder; the young Kimbangu on his way from Kinshasa to Nkamba was stopped by two soldiers in Kasangulu, the first one

(Mfufu) took Kimbangu's Nzombo (fish), = Remember that after this steal, everything this soldier was eating had a taste of a Nzombo (fish)= The second man had his chest grow breasts that were leaking water. This revelation sent a strong message, saying becareful, with this man. That this man is untouchable.

Kimbangu took the way to Mbanza Nsanda after tree months of teaching and healing people, and resurrecting the death, on the six of April 1921, Protestants and Catholics missionaries launched the Avis de Recherche against Kimbangu; He was in the wanted list. They said: The Kimbangu you have been watching is a long story that is dated far behind time. Be sure it is God Himself who is manifested in Kimbangu; in the body of a black man.

The coming of Kimbangu symbolizes peace in the world, and world in Peace. That is the new intelligence He came to give. Kimbangu is God Himself inside a black man's body in His full knowledge like discharge paper. No one else in the world has left a discharged paper including a new system of writing.

Chapter 10
Kimbangu According To Professor Coovi Gomez

I am going to summarize my entire expose for brevity. The exact title of my expose is the following:

- Accomplishment of the prophecy of Simon Kimbangu relative to the mental and spiritual liberation of black people: retrospective, perspective and prospective.
- I chose to adopt a classical plan. First a prologue titled 26th day of February 1885—to—26 February 2011, a total of 126 years of Humility and humiliation of the Congo.
- First part is: the birth of a vocation and the affirmation of a mission. It is of course the calling of Tata Simon Kimbangu and the mission he assigned to Himself.
- Second part is: Accomplishment of the prophecy and the actualization of the spiritual message of Simon Kimbangu by the ABAKO's youth.

I will end with an epilogue: Kongo Fer de lance de la renaissance Africaine?

I neither affirm nor deny. I only interrogate myself on the capacity of this geant to assume its role in the concert of nations. I would like to start with the prologue. First of all, we must know that the Berlin Conference started on Saturday, November 15th 1884 at 2:00 p.m. inside the big hall of Bismarck (the German Emperor). That conference was scheduled to last for only two weeks; but between November 15th 1884 and February 26th 1885 at 4:30 p.m., you can see how long was the conference lasts. The first conference of its kind in history that did suck and drain it feuille de Route (it is a never seen) and we saw nations hurting themselves with countries like: England, France, U.S.A., Swedish, Denmark, Turkey, Russia, Belgium, ect, ect . . . And sometimes representatives of these nations never walked the soil of Africa. So, we were in front of a comical situation where diplomats, business people, explorers, mercenaries and every sort of adventurers were dealing and busing around a map that was a wrong map of (Kiepert Map); Kiepert was a mapper who thought Africa was the continent of Pere Jean Kingdom, (a mythology of a certain imaginary Ethiopian King that allowed in his kingdom to have concentrated all richness of the Earth God had given to mankind). So, even there you can see that all richness of the world was not concentrated in the place called the "holy land" of Palestine again less in Europe, the continent by excellency in salvation mission but on the land where men are (in negligible quantity), savages, refractors to the civilization with no cultural tradition (as they portray) Africa. That is not fair. So, what is important here is the conference. Despite its exceptional time duration, (Saturday November 15th 1884 to Monday 26th of February 1885), there were eight meetings, meetings made up of panels. One meeting alone lasted two months. The one that lasted longer was the one that supposed to determine the fate of Congo. Regardless other countries, how they decided on the fate of Congo:

It is the best way; the best transition that will allow us to get in the person of Simon Kimbangu.

First meetings were presided by two men, Conte Asvelt and one advisor who had a predestined name, a certain Bush. Those meeting were becoming a place of argument between the British and the Americans. At the beginning, Belgians King Leopold did play the bench boy because the spinal cord of these meetings was the fate of Kongo and the (Basin du Kongo). According to Hasvelt, Kongo basin was the place on the earth that has much more wealth:

- Rivers;
- Precious metals.

The British lust was after Kongo basin; France did the same, and Portugal's claim to have legitimacy on the land for reason of its precociousness in the region as masters of slaves, and even Netherland had pretention on Kongo. What is extraordinary is the way Leopold ended up winning Congo (DRC). But you need to know at that époque the Kongo basin covered the south part of Gabon, large part of Angola and passing all that region, the African great Lake region to the deep end of South Africa which was called (at that time) little Kongo.

With the tought of Tata Simon Kimbangu, there is another Kongo. It is Kongo Katiopa with its sons dispersed all over the world and destined for an eternal slavery by those who say: they are acting in the name of God. Meaning the European missionaries. This is to say, we always are deeply confused between Kongo Katiopa (Africa) and the believers of Kongo with a posterior territorial fork.

So, after this precision, what I would like to say is that rivalry between Hansir Edward Malek of England and the representatives of the U.S.A. have brought the Americans to say: finally it is the international association for the conquest, exploiting of Kongo founded by Leopold II and some Belgians mostly Flemish who were asked to take Congo by hands. This is what the final act of the conference stated on the 26th day of February 1885. Bismarck who was there at the beginning, disappeared for only to come back at the closing time of the conference.

He took the word and said the following:

Misters, Ambassadors, in the name of God the almighty, I believe answering to the general feeling of this assembly by hailing and greeting with satisfaction the movement and approach of the international association for the exploitation of Congo and by taking act of the agreement made around our resolution, therefore, the new state of Congo is called to become one of the principal guardian of the oeuvre of the European civilization we have envied. And I formulate wishes for its prosper development to the benefit of the nations of Europe and for the accomplishment of our noble aspirations of our illustrious founder Leopold II.

That is how Kongo land was cut into pieces for the third time with an Independent State of Congo, a personal property or possession of the Belgian King. Not a colony yet an independent state and an exclusive domain (fief) of King Leopold II. In an other word, his hunting field, to enjoy life. We must understand that that whenever we speak about Congo; symbolic charge is something very important. When, during the ceremony of the independence of Congo, you invite the king of Belgium as a guest of honor and while the same king did not apologize to what happened in the past, it is gravissimi. This is to say the numerous deaths of Congolese victims and martyrs was not done. It is like you sold the memory of these victims; and you have killed them for the second time.

How the Vocation of Tata Simon Kimbangu was born?

It is known that every human being, regardless, has been, in the face of the world, living with some interrogations that structure and frame his destiny.

The first question is the following:
  - **where do I come from?**
  - Radical question of origin

Second question of origin:
  - **who am I?**
  - Question of identity

Third:
  - **What mission I came to accomplish on earth?**
  - It is the question about calling and the last question is:
  - **Where am I going?**
  - What will my destiny be after death? To what fate are we devoted?
  - **What is my post mortem destiny?**

Those four interrogations are not the preoccupation of all human beings. There are people living in ontological virtuality meaning they only live to satisfy physiological needs. But beside, there are those who ask these questions. And for that you need space in which you can ask these questions.

Who is Kimbangu from the Bantoue origin of Kongo?

It is certain that Bantu people of Kongo came like others from the south Saharian Africa from the Nile valley in Egypt in the great Lake regions. They are the native of the great Lakes. How do we know that? Simple, because all priests of the ancient civilization of Sudan (Meroitic or Napatean) or of Pharaonic Egypt, meaning Meroitic County; were following migratory movement South/North of superior paleotic to dynastic period. We observe that these people have a calling that was extremely spiritual.

Etymologically, Kongo, in ancient Egyptian language means: Leopard Hunter. (because Bantu languages and ancient Egyptian languages have genetic parenthood; and we must study them), it is not just hunters of leopards but tamer of leopard. The hunter goes after meat (food), but tamer means someone who knows the language of the animal world, and someone that feels possessing the animal's kingdom. So, all who were in that brotherhood have a distinctive sign since South Africa, they used to wear brotherhood of leopard men.

Today we are ashamed of these things because we claim to be Christians. But in fact a Kongo man is one who knows the codes and the signs that allow him to tame and gain the grace of a Totemic animal that is a leopard. It is a divine animal that belongs to the primordial Ancestral Spirits. For us Bantu people what we call Kongo, is the most high people and the most dignified of Africa who occupies one of the most vital territory of Africa. Thus cannot be a renaissance of Africa without Congo; because Congo is the heart of Africa that is bleeding.

How can you imagine one day the liberation of black people; spiritual liberation, mental liberation; those are the prelude of its economic liberation. Because we forget that dimension, we think as they (the Europeans) always take us to believe that it is a problem of money, buildings, or a problem of medical care and assistance, and they take us labeled the problem of development. No. Human beings need self-fulfillment. The most important thing for any human being is Dignity.

So, who is Tata Simon Kimbangu?

He is the one who brought the culture of Dignity to the Kongolese. He is listed among the people who brought solid answers to the four questions asked above. He is among those who appear only every five millenium in the circle of history evolution. In ancient Egyptian language, they call them Great Visionaries. (Grands Voyants) "Aourmawou". They do not prepare themselves by predilections of the kingdom of God to come. They are the ones who said because we have cut off ties with the values of the golden ages, that is why we are in this state. And golden age for Simon Kimbangu is Kongo Katiopa. It is the time when black people were in harmony with themselves; man or woman with him/herself, when Bantoue were in harmony with cosmic forces and divinity of nature. So, it is in that golden age that He got His initiation. Black people knew God's millennium before white people. Whites spoke about God but are incapable to act as a good man, and a man of virtues.

Africans need to understand that the vocation and the mission of Tata Simon Kimbangu, (the most old prisoner of the conscience of history of the universe; He physically died after 30 years of a life prison time), is first of all to give Dignity to the men of Kongo Katiopa (Africa), and all blacks around the world. (1921). " . . . Blacks will become whites and Whites will become Blacks)."

"Each generation must, in opacity relation, discover (find) her historical mission, to fulfill or to betray it . . . " Franz Fanon.

CHAPTER 11
KIMBANGU ACCORDING TO PROFESSOR THEOPHILE OBENGA

Thank you a lot your Grace, dear colleagues and friends. By thanking all the organizers of the International Conference on Simon Kimbangu, I would like to express all my gratitude to one another and over all to Professor Mbokolo Elikia, President of the Scientific committee and the organizing committee. Also, I would like to show all my sympathy for the highest authorities of the Kimbanguist Church and notably his Excellency here present because it is them who pursued an idea and oeuvre of supreme importance. I am happy to be among many imminent knowers of the life of Simon Kimbangu. So, we will learn a lot during this conference given the quality of occupants and specialists. I would like to insist on the following points: without being a specialist of the subject:

Who is a Great Man?

Who do we call a Great Man?

Does Simon Kimbangu, by doing his portrait, correspond to the portrait of a great historical man?

And how the liberation of black man was confused to the singular destiny of one man, Simon Kimbangu?

How His destiny has finally become the destiny of the liberation of the black people?

So, Simon Kimbangu the liberation of the black man. What are the consequences and the outcome after Him? I will summarize (as a conclusion) that in history of people in all continents, for all races and under all climates always appear, age after ages, generation after generations, if not century after centuries, great Emblematic figures; it is not excluded that such tribe, such country, such nation under the equatorial or on the north pole, have a great man; it is not excluded. We have already to put aside the idea that Africa cannot have a great man; by then, we psychologically block our shelves by thinking that we are the least of the people (in Africa). Therefore, we cannot have a great man who has influenced and impacted our history and the history of humanity.

We must come out of that sphere by not reducing ourselves and accept that we in fact have great men who incarnated by happy coincidence of many factors the changes in our lives. They have incarnated fights, hopes, and aspirations of their times because you can duel beside the line and you also can incarnate. It is that difference that make an ordinary man who incarnated aspirations and hopes. You must therefore be sensitive to your time and for many, such characters are always precursors; meaning, a man other people do not understand while alive.

Precursors, because they are not understood, or less understood when they are alive. Then they face disdain and contempt, torture and prison in the arbitrary way and they endure their passion, the suffering because they saw what everybody else could not see. Because they preceded history. They are more in advance according to the time. To superficially consider things, their lives appear to be a failure. He is galvanized, "he does this and nobody follows him." It is a life of unsuccessful because they do not even possess material wealth, they have no fortune and less disciples are counted in their daily existence. There is less that follow them. It is that the great man. However, despite material poverty, despite less social consideration, and a little audition (audience) while being alive, the historical characters bring an invincible message.

You can torture them, put them in prison, they have an invincible message and their message contains universal importance. If it was about little thing, they could dropout but the stake is so profound (deep), so universal that they cannot abandon nor give up. They are Angels who protect the society of humans. In an other word, it is to say that they are messengers, the envoys, the illuminati. They see the light while the mass is in the darkness. They are visionaries; they teach, they prophecy, they speak and guide, they heal people and make wonders. It is only later that everybody else recognize and admire their transcendence; their highest spirits and their very exceptional forces of characters. Their intelligence is out of this world, brief, they are of highest spirituality because spirituality is that element that matters most. You cannot be spiritual with a worse character, or less intelligent; how will you guide other people?

He is someone exceptional. It is that character that attracts and that we become submissive to their powerful message. Their social origin is often modest, humble but their vision of things and of the world is of a rare superiority. Their social, material outcome (offering) tells a lot more. They are poor; moreover they are devoted. So, the outcome is not their problem, they concentrate their lives to other people. Their lives become a life of devotion despite their own devotion which shows excellency and portrays a life of perfection because you need to be above everything as a spiritual man, because you are perfect. Perfection leads you up there. Their happiness is a supreme internal (inner) well. It is not visible. They speak to you in a very humbly way; they receive you even without shoes or socks, but their happiness is interior, their force is inner. It is not what is exterior that concerns them.

They incarnate in the fundamental way the gift of spirit, the gift to see things (voyance) meaning, that sublime capacity to know and to proclaim the truth almost from instinct. They do not need a school of theology but unfortunately today we have schools of theology to perfection and enhance our spirit and our gifts. But them, they have all the gifts naturally because the world and the society are their own university. What is astonishing to such rare historical characters is that their characters are radically innovator; what is in front of us its not what interest them; they want to innovate, they want a renaissance; they want us to have other intellectual attitudes, other politic, cultural ways and other spiritual inputs. Not daily banal attitudes or the compromised behaviors; half-measure, of fear, of hesitation and the fear of the gossip does not move them. They are not afraid of that.

So, to the question who is a great historical man? We can answer to the light of what we just said, that, he is a man who is engaged in his time but who transcends his time. He trespasses it. Therefore, He demonstrates engagement in the immediate and a passing of the immediate. Because of a calling that came from far away. Such is the figure of a great historical man. It must exist an historical context that is appropriate to let manifest the historical man history that is there, such it is contained already in another history; a history to come. But that history to come is already here in the present. It is their capacity to see what will happen in the present because the future is already in the present. You must be able to read it, because you can live your life history with a short conscience and with a limited spirit that does not go over above one or two generations.

We can fix the problems of one generation or two but this is a short view; you then live without guessing; without ambitions, you live without feeling the call of large to go to the large. But them, they feel it. All we speak about is the roots, the rooting, engagement in the concrete, in the immediate. We speak about all of these things, but they know that the present is urgent. We must build, educate, must do things in the present. So a great man is seized in the present by the urgency of the future.

The urgency of the becoming, it is that, his present. His present functions based on the future. Therefore, the urgency of the present foresees the urgency of the future. The two urgencies are linked. In fact, to form a one and only urgency: the urgency of life. Because you can banally live without worry of anything but them, by strongly living the present, and by forcefully feeling the future, they have the sentiment of urgency.

Can you live without urgency?

Animal, yes! But not humans. Even Saint Paul said, time urges us to build the Church of Christ; we must go quickly (fast). Do not say the others will do, you do quickly. It is the urgency of the builder. All the builders live with the urgency of the builders, urgency of the creator, the founder, brief, the urgency of the prophet. Meaning a prophetic urgency that is an elevation of the spirit. Without that feeling of the prophetic urgency, they would never be great men in history of the humanity.

Urgency that is not limited, that is linked to the immediate; an urgency that is a call to the summit; so with that they do huge things; they are at the summit of the hill. Prophetic urgency is like a powerful river which nothing can force to change the directions towards the ocean's immensity. Because, they will always lead you to something bigger; something that transcends you to the immense.

So, what immensity?

Prophetic urgency opens to the vast horizons and to the promised land, a new land of a new covenant. A new way to do things the land of all expectations; the land of election and of benedictions. The land of hope and prosperity. They give meaning to life; they extend life. This is why every great man in the prophetic urgency of his vision of the future is necessary an inspired man; a mystic almost. If we today are not mystics, because we put our knees down every fifteen minutes. But because there is a dialogue with a mission, with a message, so the social, cultural, and political forces inspire them. We are inspired by forces, by social energies. We see how people live their misery, their cultural state, their politics, we are inspired by these things. This is what pushed you; like spiritual forces push people, and let even call it divine forces. We are pushed by something, all those forces sustain us. We are sustained by these energies; these forces that transfigure you and take you to the leading position in history.

Does the very venerable Simon Kimbangu correspond to the portrait we have traced?

I believe the answer is yes.

Why Great historical men are rare and exceptional?

They are not common; they are rare; we do not have many Simon Kimbangu.

He is one of them in the history of the humanity. There are those of ethnic dimension, even the national, ethnic dimension when they speak to the nation, the ethnic dimension is no more a priority, not even necessary even when they address their familial group, all is beyond. Christ is addressed to the Jews, but He is now over the Hebrews to the entire humanity. We always need an ethnic group, a people need a region, we need of an incarnation that is concrete, charnel, historic but in long range, it is not the priority. The Jews are no more a priority for the message of Christ; it has transcended them even though they were the first to receive the message because the promised land is for everybody.

So, a spiritual dimension come from his historic root, his gift of prophecy come to him from his urgency to transcend the immediacy and his terrestrial mission is dictated to him by his total incarnation in the history of men. That is Simon Kimbangu; regardless of religious-sociological and messianic studies that reduced Him to the less. The problem is that, there is a messiah, a man of higher virtues and of extreme spiritual exigencies. He is a philosopher of well and of good; a perfect wise man; an inspired visionary. Brief a legislator because we must found ledge (the law), in Him as a liberator. You cannot be a great man without giving freedom. You must free people in order to be called a liberator. Exactly like Moses wrote the Pentateuch, explaining the genesis of the world, freeing his people (Act 7:20-23). Moses who received the science of the Egyptians; thank to that instruction, Moses was able to free his people. This is what we call a great man.

About Churches; anybody can build them. The only one thing that matters is money. But we have less Messiah, meaning the true spirit who has for bread:—the angelical sincerity (they are innocent and sincere). And they have for wine:—the friendship of the divine (you can lie to them but they don't lie).

Also, before building any churches, they know how to gather people in spiritual assembly that targets spiritual perfection and to that summit, you can finally accomplish a lot. Meaning, they are having the spirituality that is accompanied with a human project. Therefore, they are truly inspired and truly founders of spiritual assemblies before they become Churches. That is targeting spiritual perfection and to that summit, you can accomplish many things. However, it is not about any spirituality purely and simply because spirituality without précised human project appears to be an incomplete spirituality. All to contrary, spirituality to the human scale is a listening force; you must listen to others. A spiritual man is the one who listens. You must listen if you would like to change what you see. Even if it is perfect, you must do more to the perfection. You must strive to change things for the best. You are the unshakeable force of liberation; so you strive for justice, for dignity and for the salvation. Meaning, bring forward a spiritual that favors the good life inside the human community. A good life we have to live on the earth; to have at least an embryo of paradise. If in the misery there are changes, so it is rational not to have the same thing in heaven.

Therefore, we have to call it a spirituality of liberation. Like the one the Latinos call liberation theology; but the one of Kimbangu is about the spirituality of liberation.

Liberation from what? For what? In what?

To the question why He was fighting? Because He knew His destiny is the destiny of black people. His adult life, and His prophetic life, and His messianic life is entirely linked to the existential conditions of a black man in the 19 Century; so that is the situation. In the modern history, let's say from 14 to 20th Century, no human race, no group of people on the earth has suffered more than the black people in our relations with the occident, no one. It is in fact the erasing of almost the history of the black people. And the good and powerful black people want to save the rest from that sad situation; they do not give you freedom just like that, you must in fact in that history, do your measure. This long and terrible suffering of the black man in the continent and in the diaspora, need is to ask, is there someone measuring it?

This is what black people felt; it is what they saw. Black people should not live in such conditions.

Why? What kind of arbitrary?

In deed, the situation is very deep. Many do not ignore what Jean Paul Sartre said:

"6 Centuries since, between Occident (the West) and Africa, they have created a constitution of contempt. An indigenous code, of blacks and so on . . ."

So, people like Simon Kimbangu, must they continue to live and die in the frame of this constitution of (scorn) or must we radically change the course of the events for our continent. This is the situation of an extreme historic gravity; so extreme and colossal that Kimbangu had to go through. He knew it through out small jobs, and through colonial contempt, if you are weak; they cut off your harm because you did not pay taxes. He saw that through torture, imprisonment; the derision, they laugh at you as a human being. He really bears his cross. Today everyone talk about the dignity of the human rights, of course we want it but Simon Kimbangu had His passion. His passion was to free black man from the yoke of colonial mistreatment. That is the fundamental of the problem. Yes it was tragic; He incarnated a rupture; a cut and a stop with precepts, values; a rupture with occidental spirituality (if it exists one). He radically cut ties with all of those things the Europeans brought to us. So to the light of what Kimbangu did, we can learn that the liberation of the black man requires two things:

- radical cutting off (definitive rupture) with all the organized forces that single and target the destruction or the stagnation of black Africa, (by mistakenly, we, the certain elite we are cultivating that illusion that the Europeans will save Africa), it is an illusion and Kimbangu felt it long time ago. If Occident wanted to save the Africans, if it really was the case, why they have destroyed Marcus Garvey's ships (boats) that were intended to make a liaison between the African diaspora and Africa?
- If they wanted the happiness of black people, why they did not protect Lumumba, in the Congo, instead they were more worried to protect the mine of cobber of the country?
- If it was the case that they wanted black people's salvation, why a long prison time was inflicted to Nelson Mandela? All he wanted was justice to be served in his country.
- Why a very very long long prison time to Simon Kimbangu? What he wanted? . . .

- Djomo Kenyata, Kwame Krumah, all in prison why?
- If they wanted our well being, they would not put our great men in prison.

All of this because they wanted Africa to sink so, they started by destroying every person who could free Africa. Therefore, all the great African men were put in prison and then killed. What about us now? Sure, we must create our own power to avoid being victimized again. Therefore, we must invest ourselves to knowing the inspirations of the true African people. To know what is our idea; Simon Kimbangu has brought an idea of perfection to his own compatriots and to the humanity, that it. Black man must be totally free. To free people, to break the chain of the historical links with the Occident; link of friendship, cultural links, linguistic links, cooperation; in fact, these links are chains. We must cut them off right away, once for all. That what appeared. Simon Kimbangu saw that Him and His people at that time have the mathematic equation to solve.

What was that equation?

Occident has almost no natural resources; there is no cobber, nor diamond, no iranium, nor boxid; no iron, nor oil, no chrome, nor coltan, no precious wood nor coffee or cocoa; no cotton, there is nothing: that is the X of the mathematic equation. In the same time the most performing industries are over there in need of all these mineral resources to build a materialistic civilization. So, that is what justify since the 14 Century the operation that took place at least during eight centuries, the pumping and the looting of African natural wealth and of natural resources that helped to build Occident. So deeply, the liberation of blacks from the occidental yoke is by consequence a crucial problem that only great African men have diagnosed with precision and for which they have proposed solutions not of compromise but of radical cut (breaking) with the craftiness (operation), so we need to cut ties. It is a combat, a kind of combat of black men that have leaded to the creation of a Panafricanism philosophy and of the movement of Negritude with Aime Cesair.

It is the same combat that has created Kwame Krumah, the conscientious,

Marcus Garvey, Du Bois and so many other . . . Like a folklore, It is the same combat that has created Kimbangu and the Kimbanguism, this vast movement of the mass that is an Anchor in the essential by singling without detour, the liberation of the black man, which is a real problem; so to say, no illusion is here allowed. Simon Kimbangu with no university trainings, knew and understood all of these realities with a visionary clarity. Him and the other have felt that this is not the way we must live. We are far from those who minimize black people effort; from those who criticized our people without criticizing Christ. It is really the fight, the combat of liberation that drove the faithful to build schools; they obey the libertarian message by building hospitals, educational and social centers, radio and television stations, and making plantations and printing houses. They do not do that because they have money; it is because there is a strong message of liberation; an engagement, and a reflection to the light of the founder's oral teachings that is implicit or explicit, the teachings of Simon Kimbangu Himself. It is now up to us to convince the entire Africa to adopt Kimbanguism vision: Bolingo, Mibeko, Misala (Love, Consigns, and work). This is our salvation.

This mantra and this spirit of Kimbanguism that consists of building facilities, premises and elevating the spirits of the mass, must become the most important frame work not just for Central Africa but Africa in its full extension because all the religions are universal. We have Buddhism, Islam, Catholic, all of them are everywhere in the world. So, why the message that is so powerful, that was initiated by a black man does not win the entire Africa?

If it is not originated from Africa, that is another story (the Europe said) but if it does come from Africa, bias studies use to say that it cannot go far long because it is limited to one tribe or to one region. That not where our engagement and efforts should go; this is not ecumenical, nor universal in the European sense. The Occident wants always to introduce things in a bias way. But we (the Africans) must extend our Kimbangu message because it is a powerful message. You cannot liberate yourself by being weak. This message is a message of power for the liberation of black man and of always by a black man himself and then for the humanity because Africans are first of all peaceful people. If the Africans become free, they will only do good things to this humanity.

So we are not preaching solitude or loneliness in action, nor the isolation, or the neglect or reject of the others; nor tribal or ethnic closeness. We do not preach all of those extremisms. Neither Kimbangu nor Kimbanguism preach the seclusion; the locking up does not exist in KINTUADI because today we deal with world economy, or globalization, and so on, . . . Analysts show that in Europe, they are industrialized and well advanced countries; and the emerging countries, and those classified as very poor and very indebted countries; we know where they classify us (the Africans) in that nomenclature of the globalization. We know where they put black Africa. So, given the gravisimi of this list, the question is simple, are we still going to stay in that state of fragility? . . . Elections and transparency fragility; economic fragility; material wealth, water, the electricity we can't hold and achieve properly; linguistic fragility; spiritual fragility: (we recite verses and words without getting their true meanings); judicial fragility; the lack of human rights; of transparency in the freedom of speech and in institutional; alimentary fragility; security fragility (people do not eat well in some eastern parts of Africa); sanitary fragility (people die from old diseases that do not kill anymore); environment fragility . . . So, this is after all our state of fragility. We preach and build Churches, we do politics but we still are in fragility.

So those who watch us can realize and understand that we are neither emerging nor industrial country. So to say, we are poor and indebted and over exploited countries. More Africa is fragile, more Western countries maintain Africa in fragility it makes their business. That is the logic they follow: it is easy to exploit a weak and fragile people than exploiting those who are strong. This is why Occident respects the strong Asia more than the fragile Africa. Liberation is part of making your own institutions; building your future and your life, investing with your own money. Then they will be respecting you because you are strong and less fragile. So this is the key message; when the other wants your fragility, the solution to the equation is that you conquer your liberation. Yes, we know that those who fight for the liberation of Africa are badly described by the Occidental Media and press simply because they want their puppets who are there to weaken Africa and get the title of good militants.

It is not a secret, Kimbanguists are badly perceived by all the western press, and it is easy to draw a picture or an explanation; Kimbanguists are strong and wise. Otherwise, the Western will wonder about how and where they will be going to get the Coltan, Iranium, Diamond and many minerals for free. This is the problem Simon Kimbangu wanted to cut off once for all. Cut the ties, respect yourself and the world will respect you.

This bring us to say that we need to stay away from images the Western run in the media. Images that will come back to hunt us. Just think a moment; how can they say that the waste from Africa is the number one polluting waste in the entire humanity (especially from the Congo Basin) when in fact we know well that industrial waste of America, Europe and Asia are the worst. Just think that the Africans were on the earth since the beginning of the centuries and nothing was polluted. All the Westerns are trying to do now is to create a new vocabulary for the mother continent.

We very well know that all of them, Americans, Europeans are developing every day; they do not speak about durable development. Ephemeris development of Africa is not even a development; Africans have the tendency to relegate (to send) everything to the next generation. But the contrast with the Occident is that they are doing good things every day. They do not speak about durable development. This notion is so important because in order to weaken someone, you must attack and touch his/her mental, his/her intellect first. Once your intellect and your mental are destroyed including your concepts, you are paralyzed. And when the African elite is paralyzed, imagine what and how the entire continent will look like. So, that is one of the technique they use.

When those who see clearly voice their opinions, the West does not hesitate to destroy them. They have killed Matswana in the French Congo; they did the same with Kimpa Vita in Mbanza Kongo. They always denigrate, contempt Africans by teaching some of them to hate other Africans. Once succeed in that mission, the field is then free for them to operate. But when the clairvoyant Africans come to the full comprehension of the situation, the solution they put on the table is simple, take the knife and cut off the ties; even if it hurts it does not matter support the pain and do not cry. The sad part is that there is always a portion of Africans that cries.

In conclusion, we must come to the understanding that by nature or by temperament of someone, by conviction, prophetic vision, and by beliefs, that in deed, we really have an historical and a spiritual mission. We need to realize that my suffering is also the suffering of others. This is what creates the spirit of combativeness. Today, in fact in and for our combat, what are the temperaments, the visions, the historical missions, the convictions, if there are, they are too little. May be the short gains and success of politicians . . . but despite the lieu and the place, is there an historical mission that has paved the way?

Africans need strong, steady and ever lasting historical and spiritual mission, otherwise Africans will go nowhere.

Needless to ask for Kimbangu if you have your own nature; if you are being yourself; what about your tempers? Everything must change. Everything, your conviction and your prophetic vision; where all of these are leading you? Can you live without a mission on earth? It is always primordial to know that the passion of other motivates your own combat. So that is why Simon Kimbangu was a great man. A great man with the importance of all the liberators of oppressed people. It would be an insult to range Him in the scheme of syncretism. Once the Africans are totally freed, Africa will reconstruct in the humanity. But the first human right of the Africans is to build Africa.

CHAPTER 12
KIMBANGU ACCORDING TO
FATHER JEAN-MARIE VIANNEY

Kimbangu was the Divine Envoy; sent to save the Black race. He was a non-violent. We knew Him very well because we have followed Him since 1921 to His death in 1951 Kimbangu used to wear a white ribbon around His head; we hold pictures of Him. As long as you will not recognize Him, Africa would never make it through. We the Europeans have many documents on Kimbangu; you know, He was young and beautiful; He was not an ordinary man.

He was the Divine Envoy sent especially to save Black people (1997 Belgium). Kimbanguism is not a small religion. It is one of the big religions in the world that is registered among the great thinking currents; a religion such as Islam, Judaism, and Buddhism. The Bible you read is not yours, you are coming to Europe to teach us Christianity but it is us the Europeans who brought this book to you. We would like to learn Kimbanguism. (Le soleil apparaitra, Pasteur N'Kodia, 1997, Belgium).

As a conclusion to everything that surrounds the figure of Ntumua Kimbangu, we would like to say that from the Ntumua Himself, His children and grand-children, from the scientists who speak about Him to the faithful who follow and pray Him, we are all left with numerous equations that need urgent and immediate solutions in order to fulfill our mission of salvation and in order to accomplish the number one goal of the Envoy of Almighty, that is Peace in the world and World in Peace. For this, we need to become pragmatics and ready physically, mentally, and spiritually to bring about the transformation we need to have and be. Otherwise, the entire process could be apprehended and translated as a personal and professional identity crisis as we could see it here below in Solidad O'brien's writings. The other side of the medal left us with questions regarding the Europeans' attitude, are they really believers or they are only driven by blind reasoning? We are asking because they saw with their naked eyes the wonders of Kimbangu, the Envoy of the Almighty, but they kept treating Him in the degrading manners. Of course Africans were the colonized, but where is the fear of the Almighty in all of that?

CHAPTER 13
SOLEDAD O'BRIEN

Journalism

<u>"Soledad O'Brien, The next big story. My journey through the land of possibilities."</u>

I was both angry and embarrassed, which rarely happens at the same time for me.

Jesse Jackson managed to make me ashamed of my skin color which even white

chanted "biracial whore for the

feel this way. I would just laugh. Biracial, sure, whore, not exactly, white

man's media, totally! Whatever. But Reverend Jesse Jackson says, "I don't

count?"

I am immediately upset and annoyed and the even more annoyed that I am upset and

people had never been able to do. Not the kids in the hallways at Smithtown or

the guys who wouldn't date me in high school. I remember the marchers behind me

at the trial about the black youth/ kid who beat the Latino baby. The folks that

white man's media," even they didn't even make

pissed off. If Reverend Jesse Jackson didn't think I was black enough, then what

was I? My parents had so banged racial identity into my head that the thoughts

of racial doubt never crossed my mind. I'd suffered an Afro through the heat of

elementary school. I'd certainly

never felt white. I thought my version of black

was as valid as anybody else's. I was a product of my parents (black woman,

white man) my town (mostly white), multiracial to be sure, but not black? I felt

like the foundation I'd built my life on was being denied, as if someone was

telling me my parents aren't my parents. "You know those people you've been

calling mom and dad—they aren't really your parents. What?" The arbiter of

blackness had weighed in. I had been measured and found wanting.

It knocked me off my equilibrium for a bit, the first time that had happened to

me since that guy in a bar back on the West Coast pinched my butt during my

first live shot.

After two weeks of stewing, I sat upright one day and made a decision. This man

is wrong. I am a product of my own life. That's one of the wonders of America,

you have the right to define yourself regardless of what little box someone

wants to shove you in.

As a final conclusion to the value and importance of the mother we should all praise along with the figure father, in order to understand the whole message, and to deeply enlighten the readers spirit, mind and body, let's see with Gerald Massey, what was said in the Ancient Black Egypt:

> " . . . . The festival of fertilization is a survival from the far-off past when the Mother-earth was the All and the only one, to be propitiated as the giver of food. Being the Mother, she was represented by the female, who was at first pre-human, and finally human. Thenceforth woman was the living type of the mythical Great Mother, instead of the cow or Sow, the Goat

or the She-Bear; and at this festival all womankind were one in imaging the Mother who from the beginning had been the All-One. Nothing was recognized but the female, the typical organ of motherhood, which imaged the earth as mother of sustenance; the mother, who was propitiated and solicited in various ways, by oblations of blood and other offerings, was also invoked in the in the likeness of the human female to be fertilized in human fashion. She was the Great Mother, the All-One, and nothing less than the contributions of all could duty, hugely, adequately represent the oblation. In Drummond's Cedipus Jndaicus, pi. 13, there is a drawing from the Mithraic monuments according to Hyde, which shows that the seed-sowing at the festival of fertilization was illustrated in the human fashion by male, and as the female, who was represented by the women in the orgie of promiscuity. The mystery of reproduction was acted in the festival, as the vicarious mode of fecundating the Great Mother and Good Lady, by the bountiful sowing of human seed. It was a primitive mode of representing her, on behalf of whom all women kind contributed vicariously. Call it "worship", "phallic worship", or any other "worship", the supreme object of devotion at first was food and drink, which were represented by the earth in crop, the tree in fruit, the animal pregnant with young; by the Mammalia, the Water-Cow, the Sow, the Milch-Cow, the Goose, the Emu, the Kangaroo; and lastly by the goddesses and the women who represented Mother-Earth as Apt or Isis, Nin-Ki-Gal or Demeter, when the latter had been objectified in Halthor, the goddess of love, or Sekhet, the goddess of sexual communication, as divinity in female form." [31]

---

[31]   Gerald Massey, *Ancient Egypt, the light of the world.* Vol.1 (), 59-60.

Chapter 14
My Helpers

In all education the methodology or methods and means of teaching are important but the most primordial is the conception of what has been taught to you. This is why the great African writer said that: **"Ce qui se concoit bien s'annonce clairement et les mots pour les dire viennent aisement,"[32] to mean that** "To what is well conceived, notions flow clearly and the words to say them come easily.[33] We are coming back here to the apprehension of the sum you learn. With the education I have received from my parents and that of my teachers and peers, I was able to do well at school, I was able to survive with almost no financial means outside the roof of my parent.

Yes, of course I played a major role in all that I surmounted, but the basic of the education helped me to overcome every obstacle that came on my way. A distant uncle from my father's side ended up helping me in Angola; two unknown Angolans paid my fare from the airport in Italy to Termini in Rome. The Magenta Centre opened its doors to give me hospitality, father Nzuzi, the Jesuit facilitated my union with the community of the students in Rome/Italy. Father Alfred found benefactors to pay for my university studies in Rome. And let's keep in mind that during all these activities, I personally was able to earn income from working at the Vatican Museum in the Vatican and from working in the apple and tomato fields in the south part of Italy during the time of vacations.

Leaving Europe, I came to America where I was helped by an organization for refugees because of what they saw as my great intellectual potential. Finally, I came to Canada where I lived under the welfare system to the point that I received all my papers allowing me to pursue further studies and at the end to get, under hardship some good works that allowed me

---

[32] Boileau, Art Poetique.......
[33] Ibid [my own translation].

to become financially independent. God willing, I helped myself and also people helped me.

I must mention that in the course of each of these events, I did not lose track with my father whom I was corresponding with every time something was occurring. If we have to believe that in the world of spirit there is not a distance, Father was and is always with me by his intentions, prayers and wishes. That is the first reason he made me survive. The second is the presence in my mind of my sisters and brothers I have to assist financially. Yes, I became an asset for my close family, but I was also helping some new immigrants who were coming to Toronto from the Congo by providing them with bed to sleep and sometime food to transit the period they need to settle. Oh yes, many of them are here living well in Toronto, Canada. My musical Group helped many Africans to get in touch after times with their hot African cultural roots in this cold adoptive country, Canada.

At a certain point, I have to bring to Canada one of my brothers. Keeping in mind the tribulations and obstacles I have encountered and endured on my ways from Africa to North America, I have sworn to not let any of my relatives to experience similar painful and degrading situations on their ways to the new continent. I prepared the trip for my brother who landed at Kennedy airport in New York and the same day I took the plane to join him in Manhattan, where we spent a night in a luxurious hotel before heading to Toronto, Canada. Today, I am proud I accomplished one of the most important missions in helping my brother to become a well-educated Canadian with a decent job.

I know well that today every institution in the Congo is broken, starting from education to road infrastructures. The very imminent and perpetual cry you can hear from your siblings is: help, help. And you need to help them financially. You need to do that because in most of the cases anyways, giving is more inspiring than receiving. By giving, you would never know the amount of blessings members of your family and other people who benefits from your actions have been sending to you. Just recently, I met by providence a friend of mine, a Toronto Public bus driver who came from the Caribbean, whom in our conversation while he was driving the TTC bus (Public Transition Commission), asked me why did I pay the Ticket fare that day? I answered him back I really did not see you clearly because you are wearing sun classes.

So, for him, I was not supposed to pay because he was my friend. Then he told me my brother find a woman who would really love your family; he said so because he knew the challenges I was having with a non-motherland wife. Your family here in Canada as well as that there back home is the very and most important thing. Then he recalled the initiation gesture his grand mother used to impose on him. His grand mother used to ask him to always share his food with his relatives. At that time, he told me, he could not understand why. But now he knows that education was the life's blessing his grand mother was giving him. Our blessings said Father Hebga come first of all from our parents:

> Les parents sont, par le fait meme de la transmission de la vie, des etres sacres qui participent a la paternite de Dieu et des Ancetres. C'est ce qui fonde leur pouvoir de benediction, mais aussi de malediction. Les notables, mystes des grandes confreries, les chefs de famille ou de clan, les pretres, devins et autres ministres de la religion, detiennent et exercent le pouvoir de benir.[34]

> The parents are, by the only fact of the transmission of life, the consecrated beings of which participate as the paternity of God and the Forefathers. It is what melts their power of blessing, but also of cursing. The notables, priests, fortune-tellers mystics of big brotherhood, the heads of the family or clan, and other ministers of religion, possess and exercise power to bless. [my own translation]

He (my friend) even ended the conversation by saying that the work he is doing today, pays more than a PhD (Doctor). And he is, in fact, the one who provides for his entire family in and outside Canada. All of that because of the blessings of his grand mother back from the time of his infancy in the Caribbean.

---

[34] Meinrad Hebga, *Sorcellerie, Chimere Dangereuse...?* (Abidjan: Anades, 1979), 167.

There was no doubt to listen to advice like that one because I too was another example of him. Everyone lives for a reason; and one must know why he/she is living. For some, family task is a burden but for many taking care of his /her family is a must do; it is a vocation and a mission. You do not know someone well enough until you spoke and lived with him/her.

For years, my brother came to Toronto, Canada. All I knew, I took him from Africa to America and I had to make sure I am in charge of him which of course I did. But regardless of my brother tends to be selfish sometimes, act that was my day to day interrogation, remembering the fact that even in that mind set of his, he also was occasionally helping the rest of the family back home I was seeing that his help was not sufficient enough. Most of the times I had to push him to do something very lasting and meaningful in term of finance by reminding him that I Adolfo, came to America to study and to work in order to help the rest of the family in Africa. That was the promise I gave to my Uncle (from my Mother side) who paid the airplane ticket for me, and have kept the promise.

I know that my brother was listening because some times in our conversations, he will bring back memories surrounding the death of my mother and that of our last little sister. I will listen to him and learn that the pain and sorrow were there still in his inner being, and that the real reason of the quick passing away of our mother (according to him), was the worries our Mother was accumulating due mostly to the irregularity presence of our father and of course the seasonal lack of money that created and triggered the cancer that took her life. This is another point of view that is argumentative, but that has also its merits.

Beside those reluctant feelings, I was having vis-à-vis my brother, I was enlightened and moved by his deep knowledge of the history of the health's situations of our family especially on my father's side. This recount happened when we went to Varadero in Cuba for vacation and to have my brother evaluate the fiancée I was going to marry. After a trip to Havana, we came back to Varadero where in and under the oppressive heat of the Caribbean sun, my brother asked me temperature. I replied may be 30 or 40 degrees. And He continued if it is so hot in the region like this one, imagine what it would be in Central Africa. I think, he guessed, we could not anymore support the heat of Kinshasa in Africa. I just laugh.

We then moved closer to the laying chairs of one of the swimming pools of the resort. It was there at that spot that I learned that my brother was really my brother because he knew the history of the family. He explained to me why we in our family, always have to suffer from body pain. It is something we inherited from the blood of our father's family side. Starting with the big brother of my father, our uncle, to my father and some of our cousins (male and female), we all have that issue and we here in Canada are not saved from that dilemma. But all I know best is that our family produces intelligent human beings and over all we love education and we are united in mind and spirit.

CHAPTER 15
PERPETUAL TRIBULATIONS

First of all, I am born under the astrological sign of Leo. I am artistic, creative, intelligent, Leader and entrepreneur, I am the head not the tail. I am artistic and ambitious. This by the way does not define my character because I have a name and a vision that give me my identity. Through ups and downs of this life, I was followed, watched and even set out by some people of bad intentions just for my work ascension.

The so-called vicious circle in life does not exist. There is not determinism or fatalism in life. There are people who studied your path; who follow your progress to look for ways to harm or stop you. They will see your past what happened here and there, they will study what you believe in; your ancestral customs, your needs, your dreams for the future and your superstitions. Once they know what keeps you driving, they used all of those elements for one and only purpose, to unable you financially, they will create fake situations to disturb your attention and your mood. Once you fall in their traps, they ruin your career and therefore stop your dreams.

What you can do is to be quiet and keep your intentions in your inner being (inside) and react only when time is prosperous when all the conditions are reunited. Do not even share your good experiences with your co-workers, for they are the most dangerous people. And always do your work in perfect ways. Let not your mind be corrupted. Stay and be who you are. Because you know what happened with Caucasian people, among them, they talk about everything and there is no secret. But when a black person enters the scene where they are, they play him/her by hiding the truth of who really they are. So, they do not trust us. They think that as long as we remain ignorant of their business, they will be happy and dominant.

Twice, in the past at the beginning of my Teaching career in 2000 and now in 2011, my principals created problems for me when after I asked some colleagues at work about when and how to retire; the information they all knew very well but refused to share it with me. These people knew I have a popular community television program which I produce weekly. They also knew that I produce excellent dancing and very philosophical music, and they knew that I was exhaling in my studies for the Master's degree and PhD which I have to delay. The principal (a white) in concert with the Superintendent and some colleagues dragged me into a serious series of problems with accusations that would ruin my teaching career if it was not for my reflexes, my instincts and my reasoning, my faculties and capabilities of solving new problems.

Jealousy was part of that (because one of the Teachers to whom I shared the news of my admission to the Doctorate Studies at the University of Phoenix, program which I have to drop out due to the circumstances), went and told the other teachers who knew that my long term goal is to become a Doctor; also, came to the picture, the salary scale; because they also knew I was step away of becoming a principal and they also knew that in 3 year-time my salary, because of my high qualification, will equal theirs who have been teaching for their entire lives. Imagine living these experiences in a Catholic School where every morning the same principal and other will read and preach the Gospel that they do not follow and practice. It was extremely sad.

Prior to this whole fabricated issue, I remember going to the School Board Credit Union office asking them on two different occasions for a loan because I was a member and a teacher, but they refused to give me the loan I have been asking regardless of the robust of my salary. It is sad when I reflect on situations like these ones and realized on top of that that the manager of the credit union of our school board was the previous boss from my school who used to admire my talents in music and watch my television show. She was the one who evaluated me twice with satisfactory result from the evaluation system imposed to us (Teachers) by the government. Why were they afraid of me getting money? The money I could easily reimburse. And when it came that another agency outside the school Board assisted me with a loan in time of extreme needs, the board had no problems garnishing my salary to pay for the loan. Why should I look outside somewhere else when in fact what I am looking for is close there within my reach?

The other dramatic thing is the fact that my moves and activities were monitored. I had (on his request), one of the black men from the Caribbean who works for our same school board; my television crew and team knew that that guy was sent by those with whom I work for. He came to my place to do the recording, he asked to go to the washroom, I cleaned it and let him go in, then we spoke before the show he was positive in saying that Christianity started in Africa and he knew Cheikh Anta Diop and other African great figures. But when I show him some book that talk about the origin of the name of Jesus and other book on the true color of Abraham and Sarah, he was astonished and asked where he could find those book in English. In fact, we did the recording of the television program and at the end I told him that I do this work for free, and I gave him special bottle of red wine (Yellow Tale) plus $40 as gas money.

He left. The program was broadcasted on national television and the guy called me requesting a DVD of the program because many people watch it and they liked it. But the day after, when I went to work, my boss (a friend of my TV guess), defended the name of Jesus (Yoshua) she said on the PA after the morning prayers and before the end of the announcements.

> I knew right away that the guys spoke to her but they did not study Theology and they do not know the truth about religion. How "Yoshua" could become Jesus? Are we dealing with two people or one person only? And the so-called replacement Jesus in the time of the Romans was a rebel guy who was crucified and died on the cross, as always, naked. He did not even perform wonders like our African Almighty's envoy Kimbangu who gave his life and took it for the Independence of Africa and all the Blacks in the World.

I always pray that the Belgians, British and the Americans release the information they possess on Ntumua KImbangu. That fact alone will send a strong message and will unfold the Isis and the Horus, Osiris story the Europeans have plagiarized; lets me say it loud and clear: The census in the Romans Time does not reveal the existence of a certain savior by the name Jesus being born in Bethlehem or Nazareth. The argument we will sustain is the historical fact that the Tombs of all the black Kings of Egypt were discovered and exist to this day. Where is, therefore, the Tomb of Moses, Abraham, and of Jesus? And if we go further in our research the same Bible is revealing to us that Abraham and his children did not exist: Galatians 4: 22-24 (King James Bible) how in the World, Jesus as a offspring would exist? The Abraham story is an ALLEGORY.

At the end of that school year, I took a summer course, additional course, just to allow me to teach higher grades. One day during the class activities, I gave a signal to a young lady (teacher) who was not paying attention when it came her turn to participate. And to wake her up, I clacked my two fingers, this teacher and student angrily jumped up telling me in a voice full of hate, don't do that to me. All the students looked at us, and humbly I said to her sorry. At the end of the class that day, while almost leaving the classroom, the professor of that course called my name and stopped me; she said I want to talk to you. I was thinking she would talk to me about academic thing but instead she said: Adolfo, what is going on here? Why did you do that to that student (imagine we are here Teachers and adults). I answered the professor I said nothing is going on, the fingers clacking is something we do in my African culture and it is not offensive. The professor started lecturing me on that issue; simply because I did it to a white lady; because I recalled automatically doing the same thing in the same class to another student the only one black girl (we were only two blacks), who forgot her moment to answer; that time, the professor said the fingers clacking is ok, it is cultural and no one argued.

Now imagine the embarrassing mood and the stress the professor put me into the first time when white student reacted badly. If I was not strong and perseverant, I would have dropped out from that course. And I was the only one student with the Master's Degree in that class. I did all my assignments properly and finished the course with (A) as mark.

Since that experience I knew why many black students ended up becoming drop outs. The attitude of some professors and some students is not welcoming. Now the second surprise to that university was a surprise visit by television guest, the black guy from the Caribbean who one day came to the campus and I saw him there in front of the elevator waiting for me. We spoke and at the last day of school, I saw one student giving the professor the same brand of wine I gave my black fellow. Coincidence! And I omit here some issues that the professor was bringing to the classroom that really was making me feel uncomfortable but my goal was to pass the course and to get my qualification, which I did. Some blacks just work for the white people not for the advancement of their respective community of people.

Going back to the issue regarding the principal, in situations like these ones, I said to myself, the first time 10 years ago, the system got me and I had to resign because I was just starting my career in Teaching in Canada (which is mainly a white field), and I was on probation as a beginner and the union had to convince me to resign which I did but with this new problem they brought on me, now that I am a permanent Teacher, I must fight; I must stand for a fight regardless of the consequences. It was clear: if some one throws (on you) a small stone, you must reply with a big one.

As always, the first thing I did was to speak with my father. I explained the situation to him. How the principal is giving me hard time. My father asked me if I do recognize doing something wrong, I said no Father; and he told me be calm my son. If you were wrong or did something wrong you might apologize or beg for pardon but if you did nothing wrong and they targeting you just because of jealousy, believe me my son, they will not succeed, they will not win. Then my Father cursed that principal. After that I told my father that I will strongly fight for my right against this discrimination and racism act, my Father urged me to go a head. That was my blessing. It is easy here to understand how we true Africans work. We get our power from our parents.

Power is not just constitute or built objects, it can be a simple word of the mouth. And to go further, one prominent British said: **"to test a man's character [courage], give him the power."**[35] Yes, I have received the power and it was up to me on how to use it because some people use the power to spill and shed blood; but me instead I used that power to make people think and to drag them to the good reasoning process.

---

[35]   Cited by Abraham Lincoln, 16th American president (1809-1865).

My father even diagnosed the entire scenario since I came to Canada; as well as my big brother also, wondered once, how come and why they always bring problems to your life? The answer came from my Father who told me: my son, they know who you are; they know your star and your potential that is why they are acting this way, but fear not to be pursued. Just remember those who have tried to harm you in the past where are they now? And I knew well some of them are now resting in the rose garden.

I knew that this new boss had bad intention as it also was revealed to me by the Teacher's welfare agent from the Union, and I also knew that this boss was tasting the water based on the narrative of those teachers who hated me for mere jealousy; I then profoundly took the matter to the union (even unfair they might be I decided to call upon them) and filed a claim at the judicial Institution of our Province. I would really like to share with next generation the outcome of the claim from the Tribunal perspective but every leak of information is prevented, restrained and restricted by law.

To those interested, I am displaying here some of the notions the Tribunal stands for:

4.5 Employee: For the purpose of this policy, the term employee includes: full-time, part-time, temporary, probationary and casual employees, co-op students, volunteers, job applicants, staff of City Counselors, contractors and consultants working for the City of Toronto.

4.6 Equal Treatment: Equal treatment is treatment that brings about an equality of results and that may, in some instances, require different treatment. For example, to give all employees equal treatment in entering a building, it may be necessary to provide a ramp for an employee who requires the use of a wheelchair.

4.7 Harassment: Harassment means improper comment or conduct that a person knows or ought to know would be unwelcome, offensive, embarrassing or hurtful. It is a form of discrimination. Harassment may result from one incident or a series of incidents. Harassment can occur between co-workers, between management and employees, between employees and Members of Council, between employees and vendors, between employees and recipients of municipal services, between employees and members of the public, between Members of Council and members of the public, between Members of Council and their staff.

The following procedures have been established so that complaints of discrimination and harassment can be resolved internally and are intended as an alternate dispute resolution process. These procedures should be read in conjunction with the City of Toronto Human Rights and Anti-Harassment Policy. The goal of the policy and the procedures is to prevent, correct and remedy situations of discrimination or harassment and not to be punitive, although discipline may result.

These procedures do not prevent complainants from exercising their rights under other complaint avenues.

Accommodation of special needs (e.g., documents in alternate formats, interpreters, off-hour meetings) will be provided as required to ensure that parties can fully participate in the resolution process.

1. Confidentiality: Discrimination and harassment are very sensitive issues and all persons involved with a complaint are expected to treat the matter as confidential. Employees may be disciplined if confidentiality is breached. Managers and supervisors are required to keep information as confidential as possible when addressing human rights concerns. The Human Rights Office will preserve confidentiality as much as is possible and will not share information without consultation with a party to a dispute, or as legally required or permitted, subject to the requirements of a fair investigation—consult the Human Rights Office for details and exceptions.

2. Informal Resolution Options: Under the policy, several options to resolve harassment and discrimination concerns are available for employees. An informal approach can foster prompt resolution, without a formal investigation. Quick resolution of a complaint can prevent escalation and further negative consequences and is best achieved if issues are raised as soon as possible. All persons who believe that they have experienced harassment and, or discrimination should keep detailed notes about the issue.

a. **Consultation-Advice &
Assistance:** Employees may
benefit from having expert
information and advice before
deciding how to proceed with
a discrimination or harassment
concern. It is the employee's choice
as to who they seek advice from
to help resolve a human rights or
harassment concern. Employees
can consult their supervisor,
manager, director or division head;
Human Resources staff; Employee
Assistance Program staff or
Human Rights Office staff. These
staff all have a responsibility to
take action to resolve and prevent
harassment and discrimination—
refer to section 3.0 of the Policy,
Roles and Responsibilities—and
can provide advice, assistance,
coaching, and referrals to
assist employees in addressing
harassment or discrimination
themselves. Employees may
also consult their union or staff
association. Taking this step can
prevent escalation of the problem
and promote the timely restoration
of a discrimination and harassment
free workplace. All consultations
to the Human Rights Office will
remain confidential as much as
is possible, or as legally required.
Consult the Human Rights Office
for details.

b. Talking to the person about their conduct: All employees are encouraged to attempt to resolve matters themselves before filing a complaint. If an employee feels s/he has been harassed or discriminated against, s/he should immediately make known to the person that his/her conduct is unwelcome or offensive and against the Human Rights and Anti-Harassment Policy. It is important that this message be clear and unambiguous. When presented with such a concern, all employees, including management staff are expected to make reasonable adjustments to their behaviour to resolve the matter. If addressing the person responsible could lead to an escalation of the harassment or discrimination, to safety risks, or is not appropriate, employees may pursue other resolution options outlined in this policy.

c. Interventions by other staff: If an employee is unable to resolve the issue him/herself or the discrimination or harassment continues after asking the person to stop, the employee may request management or the Human Rights Office to intervene or investigate to facilitate resolution. Most complaints are able to be resolved at this stage without a formal investigation.

This option may include:

- ° a more in-depth examination of the concerns and allegations; consulting, advising, meeting with and, or interviewing parties e.g., management, the respondent, witnesses, Human Resources staff etc
- ° a review of documentary evidence, e.g., email messages
- ° communication of findings to the parties in dispute and recommendations to remedy concerns
- ° an option by parties to participate in mediation or to have a facilitated n egotiation to resolve the issues

Where the Human Rights Office is contacted, Human Rights Office staff will determine in consultation with a complainant whether the concern(s) can be referred to division management to allow an opportunity to resolve the matter.

This is an opportunity for parties to resolve a dispute, ensure the workplace is free from harassment and discrimination and address broader issues that caused or contributed to the dispute.

Depending on the nature of the complaint and the complainant's desired outcome, respondents may not be informed of a concern against him/her, i.e., where the complaint does not warrant exploration, where the complaint is outside the Policy mandate or where an issue can be resolved through a remedy such as training. However if a formal complaint is filed with the Human Rights Office respondents will be notified in writing as soon as is practicable. See Section 4.

So, considering such treatment, to the believers of Canada as a safe heaven, we must say: think, think twice and think again and again. All of this is happening to me during and after my 23 years time living in Toronto-Canada.

Now you see, our primordial goal was to tell you "how to thank your parents". The second was to show you the ambiguity of belonging of the child, being at the same time him/her self and also being the one who carries the DNA of his/her parents; if not of his/her grand-parents. We chose to show you some of the lies of Eurocentric teachings. The third effort was to provide you with the guide line or the line of conduct on how to free yourself and to bring you to the knowledge of the who you are and the what you can do and achieve. To clearly find out in whom you can put your trust especially in time of tribulations and distraction. We are not forcing you to give total faith or credit to what we are saying here.

We are simply trying to bring you to the table of a lone meditation and of research. Check the facts; do your own brainstorming based on this writing. We took the time to explain who is a woman and who she should be to a given community and not forgetting her companion, the father as the provider and the guardian of discipline and moral conduct. His character is not put away from the one of the mother, the life giver and the transmitter of affections as our common senses assert. This is universal even thought each society; each community has the philosophy of its own. There is a need here to remind people that by definition, philosophy is critical thinking (reflection) on the totality of the real. This is to say, every community has its philosophy because wherever and whenever there is a human being, there is also a vision of the world. Why?, because this human being is subject to and object to a method and tendency of thinking. Therefore, it is easy to draw the line by saying that the core of our message is universal.

Finally, the last we can tell you on this topic is to be yourself. Take your future in your hands with the blessings of your parents, physical and spiritual. By doing so, you will restore your dignity, gain respect, and move forwards the direction of a better future and of a stress free life.

CONCLUSION

In conclusion, many would speculate and think that my life (as shortly described in this book) was somehow miserable, oh not; far from that. In good and bad times, as true African, I knew how to always celebrate with joy. Since my childhood, I have been living a balanced and wealthy life considering the fact that my father was a businessman and I had a mother who was also a woman of integrity (financially and morally speaking). The sole inconvenience, my brother once said is that, according to a very long time friend of my father who is a millionaire in Kinshasa, DRC, my father supposed to be a very rich millionaire if it was not for his penchant toward women. If he did not choose the polygamist path, our entire family would be very prosperous.

But even with that social handicap from my father, we managed to grow up with decency regardless of seasonal and occasional financial ups and downs. Money comes, money goes they said. The most vivid example of my father's hospitality and generosity is the fact that our house was like a Church or a transit home for many of the members of my father's family; everybody that was coming from the village to settle in the capital, Kinshasa has to sojourn in our house. Also, every time my father was back in town, in the Capital, after a business trip, he would share sixty percent of his family groceries with the neighborhood. He would give away food and money freely to those in needs. He was really the true replica of San Antonio, as is his name Antoine Tukilonga Tekadiomona.

Today, sadly in America we hear stories of any kind of abuses from fathers, uncles and some friends, male and female. It seems like everyone wants to count the accusations from someone in his or her entourage. Many adults are merely and accidently demonized for the purposes only the accusers can explain, but let us not forget that beside this very intentionally cases of accusations, there are overlooked facts no one can deny; and for those proven cases, justice must be seized.

On my side, I will greet my father and my mother with flowers and money and the wish of a long life because if I am alive to day, if I survived all these obstacles in my life, it is because of the strength and the spiritual force I have been getting from my parents. They have prepared me since the beginning through advices and prayers and above all I carry their DNA. I refuse to be accused of giving full credit to the genetics in spite of numerous secondary factors that contribute to the enhancement of a human being and I also refuse to be accused of promoting Genetic alone. Why? because I see it (genetics) as a major element that determines a human being in his character as well as in his deeds. If allowed, I would even suggest that the judicial System implements background check on the genetic of all citizens to determine criminal disposition among people and this from the day of birth.

So, for someone who grew up in Kongo Kingdom part of Zaire, the Democratic Republic of Congo as well as the North part of Angola; we grew up with the belief that your parents are your Creators here on this earth regardless of their behaviors. And because they are Creators, listen to what King David said about how to thank the Creator:

"Offer unto God thanksgiving; and pay thy vows unto the Most High: and call upon me in the day of trouble; I will deliver thee, and thou shalt glorify me." (Psalm 50:14).

Almighty who is your father, your mother needs praises from your mouth. Praise your Father and mother. That is the best way to thank your Father.

So, to those who would pretend to think and argue that their fathers were absent in their lives and did not do a thing in their growing process, they need to see the other side of the medal. The very builder of your life is not the institution you belong to. The very maker of your life is not those who give you pay checks every second week or at the end of every month; the owner and master of your life is first of all yourself. And because you are the Master of yourself, you need to thank your father and your mother who gave you the inside and out-man or woman you are. It is because of the character you have gotten from your parents, character that is hidden inside the genes of your DNA. What makes you to be who you are and those DNA, my friends; you get them only from your parents; not from your friends, agents, managers or institutions. I am not trying to spare myself by telling you that it was proven that the DNA of all the races took their origin in the African DNA. From the British to the Chinese; from Norway to the cold people of Alaska and Russia, 80 to 90 percent of these people's DNA can be traced back to Africa. Needless to debate the Eugenics agenda according to which, blacks are inferiors people:

A common criticism of eugenics is that "it inevitably leads to measures that are unethical" (Lynn 2001). A hypothetical scenario posits that if one racial minority group is perceived on average less intelligent than the racial majority group, then it is more likely that the racial minority group will be submitted to a eugenics program rather than the least intelligent members of the whole population. In addition eugenics advocates, as humans, wouldn't support a system that could recognize them as inferior, possibly leading to a bias against people of other ethnicities, religions or other categorizations than they themselves are of. H. L. Kaye wrote of "the obvious truth that eugenics has been discredited by Hitler's crimes" (Kaye 1989). R. L. Hayman argued "the eugenics movement is an anachronism, its political implications exposed by the Holocaust" (Hayman 1990).

Steven Pinker has stated that it is "a conventional wisdom among left-leaning academics that genes imply genocide". He has responded to this "conventional wisdom" by comparing the history of Marxism, which had the opposite position on genes to that of Nazism:

But the 20th century suffered "two" ideologies that led to genocides. The other one, Marxism, had no use for race, didn't believe in genes and denied that human nature was a meaningful concept. Clearly, it's not an emphasis on genes or evolution that is dangerous. It's the desire to remake humanity by coercive means (eugenics or social engineering) and the belief that humanity advances through a struggle in which superior groups (race or classes) triumph over inferior ones.[36]

---

[36]   Internet (Wikipedia), is not a credible source but we are citing it here to make a point, the free encyclopedia.

No, no, that was the reasoning of some neophyte scientists and of some very racist people who were blinded by their proud attitude so they could neither see, nor had in hand true historical evidence and facts. In addition, they never put their feet in the soil of the mother continent, Africa. Nobody is inferior; and no one is superior since, as we said before, it was proven that the world came from one place, Africa. Cheikh Anta Diop summarizes everything in this short passage:

"Certains ouvrages tentent de repandre l'idee d'une race noire asservie vivant de toute antiquite aupres d'une race blanche, et transformant petit a petit les caracteres de celle-ci. Le contact de ces deux races des la prehistoire est a retenir comme un fait authentique, sans toutefois nous prononcer sur l'importance de ce contact, dans differentes regions ou il a eu lieu. Mais l'examen objectif des documents que nous possedons de ces epoques reculees nous force a renverser les rapports que l'on a voulu etablir a priori entre ces deux races depuis l'Elam jusquen Egypte. Les fouilles de Dieulafoy nous revelent que les premieres dynasties de l'Elam etaient de race negre. La serie des statuettes amratiennes nous montre une race blanche captive en Egype, a cote d'une race noire se promenant librement dans la nature. Le monde blanc ne s'affranchit totalement du monde noir qui l'a domine jusqu'a la fin de l'epoque egeenne qui marque l'entrée en scene de la Mediterranee septentrionale. (Pages 355-356, Cheikh Anta Diop, nations Negres et Culture, de l'antiquite negre egyptienne aux problemes culturels de l'Afrique Noire d'aujourd'hui, 4eme Edition, Presence Africaine, 1954, 1979.)."

"Some works attempt to spread the idea of a black slave living of any antiquity from a Caucasian, and slowly by slowly transforming the characters thereof. Contact with these two breeds of the prehistory is to remember as an authentic fact, without however our vote on the importance of this contact, in different regions where it took place. But an objective examination of the documents that we have of these remote times force us to overthrow the reports that wanted to establish a priori between these two races since his Elam Egypt. The excavations of Dieulafoy reveal us that the first dynasties of Elam were of Nègro race. The series of statuettes amratiennes shows us a Caucasian captive in Egypt, next to a black walking freely in nature. The white world was not completely freed by the black world that has dominated

it until the end of the Aegean time which marks the introduction of the Northern Mediterranean.[37]

(Pages 355-356, Cheikh Anta Diop, nations Negres et Culture, de l'antiquite negre egyptienne àles problemes culturels de l'Afrique Noire d'aujourd'hui, 4eme Édition, Presence Africaine, 1954, 1979.). "[38]

Finally, let's reflect with the praising song of Pharoah Akhenaten who sees his father and his mother in God the Sun:

You rise in beauty on the horizon of heaven, O' Living Aten, creator of life. When you rise on the eastern horizon, you fill every land with your beauty. You are Ra and you reach the limits of the lands and restrain them for your beloved son (Akhenaten). You make seed grow in women and create people from sperm. You feed the embryo in the mother's womb, soothing it to still its tears.

How manifold are your works though hidden from sight, O' Sole God besides whom there is none. You created earth according to your desire, you alone. All peoples, cattle and all kinds of animals, all on earth that walk on legs and all on high that fly with wings.

You set every person in his (her) place and satisfy their needs. All have food and their time of life is determined. Their tongues differ in speech and so do their characters.

The colors of their skins are different also. For you distinguished the people. How excellent are your ways O'Lord of eternity.[39]

---

[37]   My translation

[38]   Pages 355-356, Cheikh Anta Diop, nations Negres et Culture, de l'antiquite negre egyptienne aux problemes culturels de l'Afrique Noire d'aujourd'hui, 4eme Édition, Presence Africaine, 1954, 1979.

[39]   Karenga Maulana, *Selections from The Husia*, 22.

BIBLIOGRAPHY

Joseph Ki-zerbo, *Histoire de l'Afrique noire, d'hier à demain* (Paris: Editions Hatier, 1972), 39

Amadou Hampate Ba, French African author

Maulana Karenga, *Selections from **The Husia, Sacred Wisdom of ancient Egypt*** (Los Angeles: The university of Sankore, Press Los Angeles 1984), 1.5

COLLECTIF DES AUTEURS, Vies et Doctrines des grands philosophes (France: Second Editions, 1967), 335 [bold is mine].

Shaka Zulu, volume 1. Collectif Africain. Zaire.

AUTEUR, *The Instruction of Ptah-Hotep and the Instruction of Ke'Gemni.* P.26

Karenga Maulana, *Selections from **The Husia, Sacred Wisdom of ancient Egypt***, 7.

Amadou Hampate Ba, ***L'Etrange Destin de Wangrin*** *ou Les Roueries d'un interprete africain* (Union Generale des editions, 1973), 45.

Cheikh Anta Diop, ***The Cultural Unity of Black Africa***: *The Domaine of Patriarchy and Matriarchy in Classicalal Antiquity* (London: Karnak House, 1989), 28.

Gerard Buakasa, "Iitineraire d'un Nganga Simoni Makaya Ndonzoau," in 6.

Ivan Van Sertima, ***Black Women in Antiquity*** (New Brunswick—U.S.A: Library of Congress, 1984), 1-11.

Rudy Mbemba dia BENAZO-MBANZULU, *Le Proces de KIMPA VITA la Jeanne d'Arc Congolaise* (Paris: L'harmattan, 2002), 5-14.

Cheikh Anta Diop, *The Cultural Unity of Black Africa*, 28.

Carter G. Woodson and Willie Lynch, *The Mis-Education of the Negro and the Willie Lynch letter* (Washington, D.C: MAISON D'EDITION,.1933), 6.

Gerald Massey, *Ancient Egypt, the light of the world*. Vol.1 (), 59-60.

Boileau, Art Poetique . . . .

Ibid [my own translation)

Meinrad Hebga, <u>*Sorcellerie, Chimere Dangereuse . . . ?*</u> (Abidjan: Anades, 1979), 167

Abraham Lincoln, 16th American president (1809-1865).

Internet (Wikipedia), is not a credible source but we are citing it here to make a point, the free encyclopedia.

Cheikh Anta Diop, **nations Negres et Culture,** de l'antiquite negre egyptienne aux problemes culturels de l'Afrique Noire d'aujourd'hui, 4eme Edition, Presence Africaine, 1954, 1979, Pages 355-356

Karenga Maulana, *Selections from The Husia*, 22.

- K Bediako, Jesus in African Culture: **A Ghanaian Perspective**,1990;
- B Bujo, African Theology In Its Context,1992;
- MC Kirwen, **The Missionary and the Diviner, Contenting Theologies of Christian and African Religions,**1987;
- Lsanneh, **Translating the Message, The Missionary Impact on Culture**: American Society of Missiology Series No.13,1991;
- RJ Schreiter (ed.), **Faces of Jesus Christ in Africa**. Faith and Culture Series, 1991;
- Twesigye EK, **African Religion, Philosophy And Christianity**

in Logos-Christ Common Ground Revised. (RL-BR128 A16 T93 1996X . . . . 1996);

- Kyewalyanga, Francis-Xavier Sserufusa, **Traditional Religion, Custom And Christianity In East Africa**: As Illustrated by Ganda 1976;
- Diane B Stinton, **Jesus of Africa**. Voices of Contemporary African Christology. (BT 205 8858 2004) SMCL;
- GOOGLE:
- Celibacy;
- Celibacy in the Roman Catholic Church;
- Celibacy in Africa;
- Celibacy In African Christianity;
- Celibacy in African Theology
- P.Tempels, La Philosophie Bantoue, Présence Africaine, 1945

BIBLIOGRAPHY

1. Ki-Zerbo, Joseph: **Pre-History, Africa, Fatherland of Mankind** Introduction; 1945.
2. Internet: www.metmuseum.org/explore/oracle/essaylambrecht.html.
3. Nyamiti, Charles: **African Christian Studies, Volume**, 8; 12; 19,1992;1996,2003
4. BIBLE
5. P.Tempels: **La Philosophie Bantoue**, Ed. Africaine, Paris, 1945, P.15

2005

BIBLIOGRAPHY

1. **Bible;**

Gerarld O'Collins, SJ., *Concise Dictionary of Theology;*

Louis Bouyer., *Dictionnaire Théologique*

Mercy Amba Oduyoye., ***Hearing and Knowing***, Theological Reflections on Christianity in Africa, Orbis books, Maryknoll, New York,1986

Translation of Louis Bouyer (literally by Adolfo Makuntima).

BIBLIOGRAPHY

- Thomas HOPKO, *The Spirit of God, Wilton*,Conn,1976;
- Alasdair HERON, *The Holy Spirit,* M.Morgan & Scott, London,1983;
- Michael GREEN, *I believe in the HOLY SPIRIT*, Cambridge, U.K.2004
- Bible
- Missel Vesperal, 1949

BIBLIOGRAPHY

- Kirschenbaum,H.,and Land Henderson,V.: *The Carl Rogers Reader*, Houghton Mifflin, 1989.

BIBLIOGRAPHY

1. Green,Miranda,J., **"Dying for the Gods":** human sacrifice in Iron Age and Roman Europe."
2. Mahieu, Wauthier de**, "Qui a obstrué la cascade?":** analyse Sémantique du rituel de la circoncision chez les Komo du Zaire, 1985, Leuven University Press.
3. Soames, SCOTT, **"Beyond Rigidity"**: The unfinished Semantic agenda of naming and necessity, Oxford University Press,2002
4. Edward KESSLER, **"Bound by the Bible"**: Jews, Christian and the sacrifice of Isaac, Cambridge University, 2004
5. Peter Jeffery, **"A New Commandment":** Toward a Renewed Rite for the Washing of Feet, The Liturgical Press, 1992
6. Ed NOORT and Eibert TIGCHELAAR, **"The sacrifice of Isaac":** The Aqedah (Genesis 22) and its Interpretation, Brill,BOSTON, 2002
7. Eberhard BONS, **"Car c'est l'Amour qui me plait, non le**

sacrifice . . . ". Recherches sur Osée 6:6 et son interprétation juive et chrétienne, Brill, Boston, 2004
8. A.M KIERGAN, **"Washing Feet":** Historical and Scriptural View, Good way Publishing House, 2002.
9. David JANZEN, **"The Social Meanings of Sacrifice in the Hebrew Bible,"** WdeG, New York, 2004;
10. Sigmund FREUD, **"Moses and Monotheism"**,Vintage Books, 1939, Pan-Am

2005

BIBLIOGRAPHY

RUTTAN, Brian: **Microtheology. Notes on Autobiographical Theology**, Draft.—Groupe de Chercheurs: Vies et Doctrines des grands philosophes, Louvain,

Belgique, 1957.

—IRWIN, A. William: **The Intellectual Adventure of Ancient Man**, Page 8,

Univ. of Chicago/London THORTON, John K.: **The Kongolese Saint Anthony Dona Beatriz Kimpa Vita and the Antonian Movement**. 1684-1706, Cambridge University Press, 1998.

—Martin, Marie-Louise: **Kimbangu. An African Prophet and his Church**, Williams B. Eerdmans Publishing Company, 1976.

DEEPAK, Chopra: **How to know God**. The Soul's Journey into the Mystery of Mysteries, Harmony Books/New York, 2000

BIBLIOGRAPHY

1—Roger FISHER and W.Ury: **Gettins to Yes**. Negotiatings Agreement Without Giving In. Peguin Books, USA, 1991.
2—Peter L. SEINKE: **Healthy Consresations**. a systems aporoach, Alban Institute, 1996

www.ingramcontent.com/pod-product-compliance
Lightning Source LLC
Chambersburg PA
CBHW050400290526
45786CB00003B/1064